Write-up!
How to Teach Writing so that it Actually Makes a Difference

by Wendy Skelton

First published 2017

© Wendy Skelton 2017

Published by Wendy Skelton

www.wendyskelton.co.uk

ISBN: 978-1-5272-1106-3

Design and illustrations by Garry Robson (www.garryrobson.co.uk)

Illustrations © Garry Robson 2017

Printed in the UK by Colourfast

Photo credits:

Front cover image: © Robert Mandel 2017

Back cover image: © iofoto 2017

Page 02 © racom 2017

Page 144 © Monkey Business Images 2017

Page 154 © Michael Jung 2017

Page 174 © Dmitriy Shironosov 2017

Page 178 © Cathy Yeulet 2017

Preface

I qualified as a primary school teacher long before any National Curriculum dictated that we should be teaching children prescribed skills associated with improving their writing standards. This was a situation that afforded a wonderful amount of freedom as regards to what to teach. We definitely had a lot of fun with writing and the results were often madly creative, BUT... try as I might, no amount of just giving the children more and more creatively staged writing opportunities actually made much of a difference to the standard of writing that they produced in the long term. I began to feel that maybe some direct instruction in the actual elements of writing would be helpful to them, even though this was not the preferred pedagogy of the time.

This book is a response to the question what might happen if we combined the best elements of everything we have learnt about children's writing progression over the years. What if we skilled children up in the micro-elements of sentence construction and grammar but, at the same time, tapped into their natural creative enthusiasm and invited them to take on responsibility for their own writing progress, knowing that they were being guided along the journey by a teacher who also shared their enthusiasm for writing?

Contents

Introduction   05

Chapter One – The Importance of Being a Reader…   09

Chapter Two – …And of Being a Talker   15

Chapter Three – But I Don't Know what to Write about –   20
Developing Children's Confidence and Imagination

Chapter Four – Everything in its Place – Grammar and the   33
National Curriculum

Chapter Five – The Writing Toolkit – How to Make it Work   40
Every Time

Chapter Six – Scaffolding and Differentiation   58

Chapter Seven – But What about the Rest of the Time?   86

Chapter Eight – Writing across the Curriculum   122

Chapter Nine – How to Mark and Give Feedback   132

Chapter Ten – A Note about Boys   136

Appendices
  1. List of Co-ordinating Conjunctions   145
  2. List of Subordinating Conjunctions   146
  3. List of Conjunctive Adverbs to Structure Argument   147
  4. List of Adverbs   148
  5. Telling Sentences to Begin Paragraphs with Punch   149

Recipes for Writing Genres   155

Progression of Writing Skills Year by Year   167

References   175

Index   176

Introduction

The fact that a child is a good reader will not necessarily translate into them also being a good writer (although it is almost impossible to be a really good writer without also being an avid reader). Children get to be better readers by the process of reading more. This is not the only – nor is it necessarily the most efficient – route to mastery, but by practising the skills associated with reading and exposing themselves to longer and more challenging texts, they will improve.

The same does not hold true for writing – children need to be explicitly taught the skills, techniques and thinking processes that good writers use without being consciously aware that they are doing so. Yes, we need to encourage children to build up their writing stamina by gradually expecting that they will write more, but this expectation must be carefully contained within the sharply defined parameters of what they can already do and which writing skills we need them to focus on next. Otherwise, they will simply write longer texts at the same level that they have already mastered, and replicate exactly the same mistakes as before.

In order to achieve this, the first thing we need to know is exactly what each child is already good at, where there might exist some confusion, and what they might usefully be guided towards to 'have a play with' next. Having a 'play' with techniques associated with writing is crucial to the apprenticeship approach that we are fostering here: there are a myriad rules associated with making sense in the English language and about which it is our job to enlighten children. But once they have mastered them, they should be invited to treat them like a giant recipe book, mixing the available ingredients to craft the precise effect we are intending for that particular occasion.

To that end, it is crucial that we keep detailed accounts of each child's developing writing skills, using the statements contained in the body of the National Curriculum, and particularly those within the appendix concerned with vocabulary, grammar and punctuation as a framework. We need to have a clear roadmap of individual skills already mastered; those skills that are developing but are not yet fully secure; and those that are 'next steps' on the child's writing journey. It is of little matter (except for reporting purposes) what year–group or level this equates to; the value of the information is in the clarity it gives us as teachers about what we should be teaching next.

Armed with this information, we can then make judgements about which skills are pertinent for whole class or group focus, and which are better suited to small group teaching (or even better, one-to-one where we have the luxury of the manpower required for this). Teaching writing is rather like spinning plates: we need to stay focussed on exactly what is happening for each child at every moment so that we can intervene expediently and to best effect.

The intention of the pages that follow is to present a model for teaching writing that is both replicable and enjoyable; that covers all the requirements of the National Curriculum (including the pesky grammar strand); and which also fosters a sense of pride and ownership in the children. In other words, a model that encourages children to think of themselves as already well qualified as writers, wherever they find themselves on the spectrum of prior accomplishment, and equipped with a reliable and ever-growing toolkit of writing strategies into which they can dip as required.

It also, hopefully, will engender confidence that you are focussing your teaching efforts effectively and with meaning and impact for every child in your class or group.

As I write this (early 2016), standards are rising. And that is with the bar having been raised with regard to what the expected standard looks like, particularly in understanding and applying aspects of grammar. However, although this is definitely news worth celebrating, it seems that writing is still a subject with consistently lower achievement levels than reading or maths.

There also remains a gender gap, with girls consistently outperforming boys (an even more marked differential than with reading). So there is absolutely no reason to let up on the attention to detail or on the persistence of our intervention. We want all of our children to leave school as competent and articulate writers, with a positive attitude towards the craft that they can then apply both to the challenges of the secondary school curriculum and to experiencing the pleasure of easily and eloquently communicating their ideas for life. Our job then is to nurture the necessary skills and provide plenty of opportunities for practising them in a way that is constantly fresh and inviting.

Contrary to popular belief, surveys suggest that most children actually enjoy writing: 'A quarter of pupils thought that writing is cool and three quarters that it improves with practice' (Clark 2012). Unsurprisingly, children are more likely to report positive attitudes towards writing if they feel that they are already reasonably good at it. Confidence in writing has a tendency to decline with age and boys are less likely to say that they are good writers than girls.

Now might be a good moment to ask what – and who – has shaped these attitudes to writing? And so I'll finish with a question for you: do you, yourself, enjoy writing? Do you spend your leisure time writing or do you look forward to having time to spare when this might be a possibility? For some, the answer will be 'yes', but I suspect this will not be the case for many; for most the answer will be a clear 'no'. When I have asked this question previously in training sessions, maybe one person has put their hand up in a group of twenty or more. But the reason I ask the question is to throw the seed of the idea into the mix that our own attitudes to anything are bound to have an impact on the children's view of the same activity. It is easy for most of us to share a love of books with children when this is also a genuine passion for us.

It is also more likely that the children will see us in action as readers – whether reading for ourselves or to the class – than engaged in a sustained writing task. If we are to encourage them to view themselves as apprentice writers, then it is essential that the apprentices have a skilled master of the craft (you!) from whom to learn: they need to be exposed to constant modelled and guided demonstrations of the skills they are learning being applied in a real and meaningful writing context.

This has two main implications. Firstly, the ceiling of a child's achievement is influenced not only by the expectations of, but also by the skills and understanding of the person teaching them. If you find yourself teaching at a level that is beyond your own natural comfort zone in the subject (not an unusual situation given that primary teachers are expected to be masters of all curriculum areas, not just those in which they themselves are specialised), then I suggest you invest in a good technical book, particularly in the aspects of grammar, or read carefully the glossary of terms supplied at the end of the National Curriculum document.

Secondly, if writing is not a natural pleasure for you, this is not necessarily a problem. But you will need to put on your actor's hat for presenting shared writing activities with the children so that they do not inherit a view of the activity that translates it into a 'chore', or something that is somehow inherently 'difficult'. Moreover, it is interesting to note that when teaching at higher levels, most writing that we would produce in a real context is functional rather than 'writerly'. This means that in order to elevate the standard of class writing in general, we need to have a view of writing as being a 'craft' in which we are actively engaging and sharing the tricks of the trade with our young apprentices.

How to Use this Book

I suggest you begin simply by reading the whole thing; not with the objective of taking everything on board in one sitting, but just to get a feel of the many and various elements that influence the emergence of all-round competent and confident writers. Setting up the scenario to nurture this involves detailed analysis of how our teaching time is already prioritised and planning how this could be made more effective by laser-focussed targeting of learning objectives broken down into manageable chunks. This will result in two main 'prongs of attack': 'what will my dedicated extended writing sessions look like?' and 'what areas of writing development need regular and quick-fire practice sessions outside of my dedicated writing time?'

Then take a look at the extended writing lessons in your medium-term plan. How many? How long? What genres are to be covered? Are these based on a replicable writing process with which the children are completely familiar? Where are my opportunities for promoting real learning – not just at compositional text level but focussing on micro-skills associated with making good vocabulary choices, applying conventions of grammar and punctuation, and extending and combining sentences? Finally, you will need to look at the provision in the rest of the timetable for covering mini-sessions on SPaG preparation where applicable; spelling and handwriting (see below); and five-minute games designed to promote confidence in children's ability to analyse critically and to play with the various elements of writing in order to achieve a different effect.

A Word on Spelling and Handwriting

Although both spelling and handwriting are aspects of the mechanical writing process and contribute to the assessment criteria, it is not part of the remit of this book to suggest how you should present these. Our main area of interest is concerned with elevating and refining the content of what is written.

Children need to know how to spell both phonetically regular and 'tricky' words, i.e. words containing at least one part that does not conform to accepted phonetic rules (and there are frustratingly many examples of these in the English language). An inability to do this will seriously impede their ability to communicate their ideas to a third party.

Moreover, children also need to be able to write using a reasonably fluent, clear and joined hand as, again, it means their ideas can be decoded by an independent reader. It also ensures that their ideas can be recorded in a reasonable amount of time (i.e. before the writer forgets what it was they wanted to say). And there is evidence that being able to write in a good, cursive script has an impact on successful spelling.

There are plenty of good commercial programmes available for teaching both of these strands and, more than likely you are already using something that is doing the job efficiently. Suffice to say that it is important that the children are given continued practice in both of these skills (for spelling, the common graphemes need to be taught and analysed for patterns if they are to have any impact – not just sent home as a list of words to memorise), and that this practice time happens outside of the main literacy lesson.

Chapter 1: The Importance of Being a Reader...

As I have mentioned, it is simply not possible to become anything more than a mediocre writer unless you are also a keen reader. Although functional writing skills can be taught in isolation, the dramatic difference between a piece of writing that 'does the job', but is frankly rather dreary, and a piece of writing that is fresh and 'writerly' with a confident writer's voice and a quirky or authoritative style, can only be achieved by repeated exposure to the work of other writers who are more advanced in the writer's craft.

Writing is a considerably more sophisticated skill than reading (and it can be a source of great frustration when children's writing results do not mirror their reading achievement). Children can read more complex structures and assimilate more sophisticated vocabulary choices than they can produce for themselves. To begin with, they must be given the opportunity to hear stories read aloud to them. This is still important for children who have already mastered the act of decoding and basic comprehension when reading independently as it is an opportunity to be exposed to and to discuss writing at a higher level than they might access for themselves. They can also experience writing of a style or genre that they would not have chosen themselves. And, of course, they must be encouraged to read independently as widely and as frequently as possible in order to experience a full range of styles and genres.

Reading texts by other writers provides an opportunity to understand narrative structure, particularly in regards to how a longer text is 'glued together'. It also provides a chance to deconstruct general aspects of the author's craft – e.g. characterisation, how to create mood or atmosphere or how to manage pace; to analyse vocabulary choices and sentence and grammar structures; to imagine what if something in the story had been different; and to shamelessly lift ideas for our own writing (e.g. new vocabulary words or exciting ways to begin a sentence).

Simply being exposed to writing that is of a higher standard than the children are currently producing for themselves will, eventually, impact to some degree on the their writing standards by the natural transfer of ideas. But we also want to guide the process so that improvements happen sooner rather than later, and in a controlled and predictable way.

When Children are Reading for Themselves

Encourage them to work out the exact meaning of unfamiliar words using the context clues in the sentence or text around it: this will encourage careful scrutiny of an author's word choices and of the subtle nuances between words that have a similar meaning. Older children / more competent readers can also ask 'why did the writer pick that word and not another similar one?'.

Remind the children to stop at frequent intervals and ask themselves 'what just happened here?' This will improve their memory for retaining the main train of events in a story (and thus being able to create a sequence of related events for their own stories), and check their understanding of what is going on (many children lose coherence in their own longer pieces of story writing because they do not have the discipline of constantly checking back that the action they are currently describing relates to the action that has gone before). For older children / more competent readers, they can add in the variation of: 'why did that happen?'. Being able to see that previous actions have consequences for the ones that follow is an essential part of understanding complicated narrative structure.

Encourage children to play the 'prediction game' with the author. All actions have consequences, so can they guess what the consequence of what they have just been reading about might be? This is an appropriate question to ask at the end of chapters or where an unexpected action has just occurred. Older children can then have fun realising that better stories often include 'red herrings' – something that the writer has dropped in deliberately to mislead the reader, and the action then moves in an unexpected direction. This is the writer playing a game with the reader to entertain them.

Also, encourage the children to look for places where the writer has 'shown not told': being able to imply something that has happened or some aspect of characterisation by describing what this looks like rather than directly telling the reader the information.

For example:
Writing 'Millie hurriedly stuffed the letter back into the envelope as she saw me come into the kitchen; her eyes were red and puffy and, sniffing loudly, she wiped her nose with the back of her hand', is a better way of saying what is going on than 'Millie was upset about the letter' or even 'Millie was devastated by the letter'.

I would also strongly advocate that you encourage children to keep 'word books' (or 'writers' top-secret notebooks' or some-such). These are for recording vocabulary words or choice phrases lifted from their own reading that they will then be encouraged to use in their writing. Do not arrange these like dictionaries as the purpose is for words to make the transition into writing. It would be a rare occasion when a child needed a word beginning with the letter 'd' for example. Instead, arrange the sections into word classes such as: powerful verbs, synonyms for 'said', adjectives, adverbs of manner, adverbial phrases to begin a sentence. In this way, the books are a real resource for writing and the new vocabulary is much more likely to transfer across. Explicitly reading texts with a writer's eye also reinforces the notion that the children themselves are writers every bit as much as the author of the text they are reading.

And, of course, don't forget to reward the children with positive marking comments when you see the adventurous words and phrases start to transfer into their own writing efforts.

Obviously, it is more difficult to keep track of children's thought processes when they are reading silently, or even trickier to monitor when they are reading at home. But by incentivising the above reading behaviours (giving out points or stickers if a child can tell you about a word they worked out for themselves, or can give an example of 'show not tell'), you are creating a positive model for the children to transfer to their own reading behaviour.

If you have reading diaries, where the children record their home reading, it is also possible to add in extra columns so that they can remind themselves of examples of the above. But note that the behaviours listed are hierarchical: it might be enough for a young child or beginner reader just to tell you about a new word they have learnt or what happened in the story, whereas a more experienced reader can delve deeper into nuances of meaning, including making inferences.

During Shared or Guided Reading

In independent reading, we have to wait until after the event to question children about what they noticed. But shared or guided reading time can be an ideal opportunity to nudge the children to notice aspects of the writer's craft, because we can ask the questions while the reading is still taking place. Stop on occasions to guide discussions on word choices (why did the author pick that word rather than, perhaps, another more obvious one?). Favourite words could be added to a class 'word wall' with incentives for remembering to use them not just in writing but also in general conversation (imagine the fun in trying to slip an obscure word like 'scrofulous' into an everyday scenario). You can also stop to discuss inferred meaning (flag up that the writer has 'shown not told'); to recap the events (particularly to make the connection about why something has happened – we want the children to be making links between consequences and inciting incidents); and to make predictions about what might happen next as a result of what we have just read.

At a level that matches the children's stage of reading competency, draw attention to general aspects of the author's craft, for example, characterisation. Children often get stuck on describing what a character looks like, but in what other ways do we learn about a character? It may well be that his appearance has something to do with his general characteristics (a grubby face, torn clothes and hair in tufts might imply that the character has a sloppy attitude to his appearance or it might be that he or she was forced to spend a night in the woods when generally his or her appearance would be immaculate). Details about how the character behaves, how they talk to people and how other characters talk to them will give us a much more rounded picture of what they are actually like (much more so than saying they had brown hair, glittering blue eyes and a red and yellow striped jumper).

Use this time also to draw the children's attention to techniques that a writer uses to create a mood or atmosphere or to manage pace. Generally, long, languorous descriptions with plenty of adjectives and long sentences create a feeling of slowness. This might be enhanced with features such as figurative language (simile, metaphor, personification) or alliteration (particularly 's' sounds) or onomatopoeia, all of which would add to the general effect the author is trying to create. On the other hand, short, simple sentences (Josh ran.), exclamations (Help!) or fragmented sentences (Over here, quick…) all add to a feeling of tension and excitement and hook a reader into making an emotional investment in the fate of the characters.

This too is your opportunity to draw the children's attention to sentence and grammar structures within the text or features of text organisation. Why has the author chosen to use a long sentence here and follow it with a short one? Why has he or she started the chapter with a question or ended it with an ellipsis? What is the purpose of the information in brackets? Why are they telling us about something that happened a long time ago?

Notice features such as: the use of embedded and relative clauses to add extra information; adverbial phrases that tell us where, when or how the main action is taking place; complex sentences joined by subordinating connectives that tell us more about what is going on in the main part of the sentence. And draw attention to writer's tense choices: what is the difference between saying that 'the children played on the swings' and 'they were playing on the swings' or 'they had played on the swings'? Or the difference between 'I will visit you tomorrow' and 'I might / should / could visit you tomorrow'?

The point of these discussions is not to labour the content of the National Curriculum (although you are of course meeting the requirements set out here at the same time), but to engender in the children the notion that writers have choices about the vocabulary that they use and the sentence structures that they construct, and they pick exactly the right combination of words to create the intended effect. None of this is random.

Actively pay attention to punctuation when reading, and point out to children that its purpose is to guide you through the text and tell you how to read it. Always encourage the children to use a full range of expression when reading aloud (you will probably have to train them how to do this), as this has been proven to deepen their connection to what is being read and thus enhance their comprehension of it. As a side effect, they will also eventually be rereading their own compositions with expression that will highlight any flaws or inconsistencies in coherence.

Stop often enough to keep the interrogation of the text alive, but not so often as to disrupt the flow of the story. You will need to make a judgement here about what is appropriate for the attention span of your children based on the length and complexity of the text you are reading.

By having these sorts of conversations with the children you are, by default, training them to have similar conversations in their heads when they are reading independently. You may not see the results immediately, but eventually you will notice that they are approaching their own reading with a similar analytical mentality.

After Shared or Guided Reading

After reading, it is important that children can retell the story they have just heard or read. This ability to précis or summarise is the inverse skill to being able to plan – to pick out the main things that happened without the embellishment of extraneous detail. If the children's mechanical writing skills are adequate (i.e. quick enough), they can fill out story maps, listing in note form the main events of the story, who the characters were, and where and when it was set.

If their writing skills are likely to slow down their thought processes then you can scribe on the board in response to the children's input. In doing this, it is vitally important that you do not write in complete sentences – use key words and phrases only, the minimum information necessary to list the main events. This is because one of the main impediments to children's planning is that they do not do it quickly enough – they get bogged down in trying to write complete sentences and, without meaning to, they end up writing the first draft of their story rather than just jotting down the plan for it.

After the story map has been filled in with sufficient notes to act as an aide-memoire, the next part of the process is to retell the story events orally. This time, you do want to be encouraging the children to speak in complete sentences. Writing a précis of a story is a very high-level skill, but if you have children who are up to the task, encourage them to do this as part of the process of writing a book review for books they have read at home (a review is a précis to which they add comments about what they did or did not like about the story, what they thought worked well or did not work well and, sometimes, reference to the theme or message of the story).

Ask open-ended questions about the things that happened (particularly if you have not actually come to the end of the book by the time the reading session finishes). Again, you want to be concentrating on analysis of narrative structure and of characters' motivations: why did something happen or why did someone do that?

Remember you are reinforcing the concept that all actions have consequences. This is a much easier way of tracking narrative structure than simply identifying that a story has a beginning, a middle and an end. Children 'get' that a problem is usually established at the beginning of a story and that some kind of resolution (though not necessarily a solution) is reached by the end. But they can get lost in a mire of non-direction and incoherence during the middle part of their writing, which also makes it difficult to construct any more sophisticated ending than to resort to 'and it was all a dream' in order to breathe a sigh of relief and finally put the pen down.

Getting the children to make predictions about what might happen next is an extension of the same concept. And remember that predictions cannot be wrong at the point of making them: they can only be more or less likely based on the evidence of the events (including the micro-events) that have occurred so far.

Here again, you are encouraging the children to speak in full sentences (as this is a rehearsal for being able to write in full sentences), and you are looking to extend and develop the children's responses by prompting them, for example, to provide supporting evidence for their first statement or to give extra detail about it. Children's first drafts can generally be greatly improved by extending the sentence structures and including more detail.

If you have finished the reading, challenge the children to imagine 'what if…?' What if the Dursleys actually liked Harry and were supportive of his magical talents? What if Matilda's parents had thought their daughter was clever? What if the slipper did fit one of the ugly sisters? Again, this activity encourages the children to make links between all the story elements: if one element changes then everything that happens afterwards will also be different (actions have consequences and repercussions). This activity can be a fun and thought-provoking prompt for a writing task in its own right, but the real value is in the thought process, so doing this on a regular basis (as an oral activity, which takes less time to complete) is just as valuable for training the children's evolving writerly minds.

Finally, don't forget that discussion of films and DVDs that the children have watched (using all the devices listed above) is an equally good preparation for the understanding of narrative structure. Films usually have a very clearly defined inciting incident which happens about ten minutes in (the event that establishes the main dilemma of the plot, which the main character or hero will then try to resolve); things usually get a lot worse before they get better (most films follow a five-act structure rather than a simple three-act structure and each act normally ends with an escalation of the main problem); and there will almost certainly be a dramatic climax to the action just before the resolution occurs. Discuss how the screenwriter hooks the viewer and keeps them invested in what is going to happen in the end. A story is a story: it doesn't matter in what format it is presented to the audience, the skills required of and challenges presented to the writers are exactly the same.

Chapter 2:
...And of Being a Talker

To quote the National Curriculum document: 'English is both a subject in its own right and a medium for teaching ... pupils should receive constructive feedback on their spoken language and skills'. This is because the quality and variety of language which the children hear and speak will directly impact on their writing output (how often do you pull your hair in frustration when your pupils write in exactly the same way that they speak, with all the associated inaccuracies of syntax?).

In the same way that writing is underpinned by a solid foundation in reading, both reading and writing are underpinned by a foundation of talk. This puts us at a considerable disadvantage when children come from backgrounds where talking at home and with peers either does not happen in English, or simply does not happen at all (passive entertainment in the form of TV and computer games has a lot to answer for in children's oral language development). Indeed, a survey by the Basic Skills Agency in 2003 showed that half of teachers assessed their new intake of nursery pupils to be unable to speak audibly, to be understood by others, or to follow simple instructions – and the probability is that this situation has not improved. If these children are to stand any chance at all (in life, let alone in promoting their development as writers), they need systematic and early instruction in how to talk.

For this reason, our limited time of influence whilst the children are in our care is of vital importance. All children will benefit from repeated exposure to good models for speaking and this is too important to be left to random chance. It is our job as teachers to seek out opportunities for interacting with younger children (and guiding our Teaching Assistants to do the same) – whilst they are engaged in art, sand-play, role-play or whatever – and guiding the conversations, mindfully offering useful vocabulary for describing what is going on, rephrasing children's talk into complete sentences and asking open questions that leave room for a child to give more than a one-word response. Unless children are explicitly taught how to organise their ideas into coherent sentences, selecting appropriately from a range of possible vocabulary choices, they will not develop this skill to their fullest potential simply by a process of osmosis.

Once children leave the Foundation Stage and begin seriously to embark on their journey of writing – applying the skill of making symbols to represent letters and words that communicate more complicated ideas, by means of developed sentences that flow in a coherent and pleasing sequence, and that refer backwards and forwards establishing links between concepts – they need to be absolutely proficient in talking. They need to be confident in using complex sentences containing several layers of information in an oral context, knowing the difference between standard and non-standard English and when it is appropriate to use either of these. They need to be able to talk clearly and coherently and to extend their ideas as they speak. Obviously, this is a skill that we will be carefully feeding and developing throughout the remainder of the children's time in primary school.

We all know that a large part of our job description is to ask many questions of our pupils with the intention of promoting talk, but research has shown that although teachers do this, the format of these questions is often of a kind that invites closed answers (one or two words with little or no room for development), followed by an evaluative statement from the teacher that effectively shuts down the discussion.

For example:

 Teacher: What is our planet called?

 Child: The Earth.

 Teacher: Yes. Well done.

At all times, children should be encouraged to answer questions in full sentences. Give a sentence starter if necessary to prompt this response. For young children, you may need to repeat back what they have just said, but reorganising the words into a clear sentence.

For example:

 Teacher: What is our planet called? ... Does anyone know the answer?

 Child: The Earth.

 Teacher: Yes, that's right – our planet is called the Earth. Can you say that back to me? Our planet is called...

 Child: Our planet is called the Earth.

 Teacher: Well done, our planet is called the Earth. I loved that you put that information into a complete sentence for me.

It is vitally important that children both hear examples of and get the opportunity to rehearse organising ideas into sentences wherever possible so that this can translate automatically into their writing. When writing with beginners, always get them to say their sentence aloud to themselves before committing it to the page (this also works for good writers if they 'say the sentence in their heads' as they are writing it). This technique helps children to clarify their thinking and organise their ideas.

Always challenge children to extend their thinking and to justify their ideas in discussion. This is one of the biggest influences on their later ability to write complex sentences that include several layers of information all relating to the subject of the sentence. If necessary, you can extend the child's first answer by developing it with extra information (building on the core of the sentence that they provided in the first place). In the same way, children should always be encouraged to challenge and develop each other's ideas in the context of partner or group discussions.

The teacher could extend the previous discussion by asking a question such as: 'I wonder why our planet is called the Earth?' Question words such as 'why' or 'how' tend to invite more in-depth discussion of a topic, as do questions that ask for a child's opinion about something or ask them to make a hypothesis about something (what do you think might happen if…? What might happen next?). As various children contribute ideas to the discussion, your job is to model putting the various responses into one sentence, layering the clauses as extra information is added.

For example:

 Teacher: I think our planet is called the Earth because there is a layer of mud under our feet, which is why you might think of earth, and also, it could be called 'the' Earth because it is the only planet that we live on – otherwise we would say 'an' Earth.

Drama and Role-play

Acting out scenes, either from a known story or an imaginary one, is good preparation for writing such a scene. When children are in role, encourage them to get inside the minds of the character they are playing, speaking with appropriate register and, if applicable, with the characteristic speech inflexions of the character. Noticing and paying attention to this when role-playing is an excellent rehearsal for translating these identifying idiosyncrasies into their written portrayals of characters, giving each a set of defining qualities which sets them apart from the other characters.

An extension of the previous activity is hot-seating, where a child takes on the role of a character from a book they have been reading and the other children ask them questions. The child in character must stay in character as he or she answers and maintains a conversation (you will probably need to model how to do this before a child takes on the role). This is not only a good exercise in characterisation, but also great preparation for being able to maintain point of view – one of the things that frequently trips up unsuspecting writers when they begin their writing journeys.

Talking Like the Queen

If children's 'street' language is reflected in the quality of their written language ('we was going down the shops'), then they must be taught to speak standard English as if it were a foreign language (and to the children, it might well be a foreign language if their daily experience is not hearing standard English most of the time). Explain to them that their normal language is perfectly appropriate for general conversation, and is part of what defines them, but for answering questions in the classroom and for formal writing tasks, then standard English is the expectation.

Spend five-minute starter sessions talking to children in an exaggeratedly 'posh' voice and get them to respond in the same way. Once they are enjoying this (and they will), start to make deliberate mistakes, still 'talking like the Queen' ('Philip and me was walking the corgis down the park last night...') and challenge the children to correct you. After all, children love nothing better than catching you out making a mistake.

If children persist in transferring their spoken language constructions to their written ones, inviting them to read aloud what they have written in the voice of the Queen should highlight where corrections need to be made in a humorous and non-threatening way.

It must also be said that in the context of classroom discussion, standard English needs to be encouraged as the norm, and if children make syntactical errors they should gently be corrected, repeating the sentence for them with the correct syntax. This is not giving the message that 'street' language is wrong or inferior; just that it is not the appropriate language for a classroom setting (because if we allow it to be, then we are seriously disadvantaging these children when it comes to having the quality of their writing judged). And then the children will have a massive advantage for writing dialogue as they can discern the difference between what is the appropriate register for formal writing and what is authentic characterisation in the voices they choose for their characters.

Word of the Week

It is not possible to overstate the importance of adding to the children's repertoire of spoken vocabulary. It is a key factor in the difference between turgid writing and interesting and exciting writing. So consider presenting a 'word of the week' every Monday morning. This could either be taken from the class word wall or from one of the children's word books. The more obscure and ridiculous, the more fun you will have with it.

The challenge is to slip the word into everyday conversation as many times as possible during the week, and points can be scored whenever a child is heard to use it (preferably in a correct context, but even a close stab is worth recognition). For example: 'what a splendid jam sponge that was at lunch'; 'I think James has made a splendid effort with his maths this afternoon'; or 'that's a splendid picture of the hamster, Candice'.

Discussion Topics and Debating

Many children struggle to extend and organise their ideas on a single topic, i.e. the muscle that gives them stamina in this area is insufficiently developed. Encourage the building up of this muscle by providing topics for the children to discuss, whether at home, in the playground, or in designated class time (but preferably in all three).

A simple way of organising this is to provide a box containing slips of card with discussion topics written on them (e.g. 'children watch too much television' or 'owning a pet is irresponsible in a city' – you need to decide what level of controversy is appropriate for your children). Children then pick a topic (individually, in pairs or in a group) and explore it until they have formulated a viewpoint.

This can be extended by encouraging them to take discussion topics home to debate with their families: children who engage in quality talk at home very quickly outstrip their less-fortunate peers in terms of writing achievement at school. If the children's first language at home is not English, they will still benefit from extended discussion in their home languages as the skills of structuring debate and extending and expressing ideas are being exercised regardless of the language of delivery.

In the same vein, many schools have risen to the challenge of establishing debating clubs. These have been shown to improve results in national tests and generally elevate standards of presenting written argument. They also have the side-effect of boosting children's self-esteem as they learn techniques for expressing themselves in a way that is both appropriate and valued.

It might be reasonable to assume that just because a child can argue a point with determination and relentlessness, they would be intuitively good at debating. But actually, the skills required to be a successful debater are more subtle and require teaching. A good debate is more than just an argument; it requires the ability to see a proposal or an idea from various perspectives (useful for understanding the writer's craft of viewpoint), and the ability to listen to counter-argument and respond appropriately (cohesion of presentation).

A good debate has four separate components, all of which transfer directly to the written arena:

- reasoning and evidence – using facts and statistics to present a persuasive argument
- expression and delivery – using tone of voice, vocabulary choices and body language (in the written format, think use of capital letters for emphasis, etc.)
- listening and responding – using what you hear (in writing, anticipating what you might hear) as a basis for a creating a convincing response
- organisation and prioritisation – knowing how to structure an argument and when to present or reveal the various elements

All these elements have a direct knock-on effect in the classroom as children learn to structure their thinking and build their confidence in expressing themselves clearly and assertively. Benefits are also apparent when we consider that a large part of the writer's skill is bound up in being able to write for a perceived audience: being able to adapt language and tone of presentation to appeal correspondingly is an indicator of a confident and adept author.

Chapter 3: But I Don't Know what to Write about – Developing Children's Confidence and Imagination

Very often, it is not the children's technical ability to write that is holding them back, but the fact that they simply do not know what to write about. Their minds become a blank when faced with a clean page (a condition with which I'm sure we are all familiar to some extent). For children who are already good writers, writing a story provides them with a real showcase to exhibit their full range of skills. But for children who are less proficient, it is much easier to scrape a competent performance crafting a solid but unexciting piece of non-fiction text than it is to tackle a story. A story tends to need to be longer in order to go anywhere, making it much more difficult to retain the coherence of the whole piece, and there are too many variables involved: its limit is the imagination of the person crafting it.

For some time now, teachers have been noticing that children's imaginative skills when coming into school seem to have 'dropped off'. This may be the result of them being exposed to passive forms of entertainment when very young, rather than being encouraged to create 'make-believe' scenarios with other children. In the light of this, we will have to take counter-measures to promote a healthy imagination muscle.

As a general rule, the more we can promote creative drama and imaginative role-play, the more confident the children are going to become at making up stories (a story is, after all, simply the written form of a new scenario). If, for example, the children are struggling to come up with a new scene for a known story in response to a writing prompt, allowing them to work out the scene by acting it out first is a good preparation and confidence boost. And even if a written activity is not the intended outcome, acting out new scenes for stories as a fun activity for its own sake develops the children's creative health in an enjoyable and constructive way.

When modelling for shared writing activities, always talk about your own thinking process for selecting ideas about what to write about (you will find more on this in the chapter that describes the writing process). You want to promote the idea that all writers have to cast around for ideas, rejecting some as not being sound enough and hooking onto others that warrant further development.

Being realistic, we rarely tell children just 'to write a story'. At the very least, the topic or genre is usually predetermined. Or we might be building on a story we have already read, or, perhaps the opening scene might be provided for them. The more you can share of your own thinking process around selecting ideas to write about and then fleshing them out with a modicum of detail, the more equipped children will be to do the same.

When practising generating ideas for writing, it is not always necessary to have a full-length piece of writing as the end goal. Sometimes, a few lines to get the creative juices flowing will suffice. So will conducting the activity orally or as a shared writing practice with you as scribe.

It is better to spend twenty minutes producing a high-quality result that excites the children in the execution stage, rather than overwhelming them with the expectation that they will have to write pages at every sitting (and as we know, the quality of children's writing usually falls off after a certain amount has been written). Yes, they will have to produce extended writing pieces sometimes in order to increase their writing stamina, but most of the time, if they can write a high-quality short piece, then given enough time they can replicate this for something longer.

Below is a selection of activities both written and oral that have worked for me in the past, and I invite you to use them as a menu of options.

Creating a Bank of Characters and Settings

- Collect pictures of people and places (indoors and out) from magazines and distribute them.

- Children then collaboratively write words and phrases on their whiteboards that the picture inspires in them and then extend these to form noun phrases with one or more adjectives and extra details added about the person or place.

  If writing about a place, they should endeavour to touch on more than one of the senses for reference (e.g. what it looks like, what it sounds like, what is smells like, how it makes them feel); if writing about a person, they should include details about their family, their friends and their personalities and special skills or talents, and not just the things they can see.

- Together, they can expand on these to create written descriptions. These should be stuck on a piece of paper along with the original picture and kept in a writers' folder available for that table when the children are stuck for characters or settings for their stories.

- Some of the settings should indicate that something has happened there (e.g. a ruined building).

- You will probably want to spend some time modelling and guiding this process before letting the children tackle it independently.

A Series of Plot Twists (Fortunately… / Unfortunately…)

- The point of this activity is to build on the children's ability to sustain a narrative with events, either fortunate or unfortunate, building on what has happened before.

- You provide the first scenario for the story (e.g. a princess sets out to slay a dragon).

- The first partnership needs to say what happens next, beginning with the word 'fortunately' (e.g. fortunately, she meets an old man who tells her where a dragon is to be found).

- The next partnership provides the next story event beginning with the word 'unfortunately' (e.g. unfortunately, the princess got lost).

- The story builds up with the repetition of a fortunate event followed by an unfortunate one (e.g.: Fortunately, the princess met a handsome prince with a map, he offered to go to the dragon's cave with her. Unfortunately, the prince turned out to be very tiresome. Fortunately for the princess, he lost his voice. Unfortunately, a goblin stole the map leaving them lost in a wood. Fortunately, an old woman invited them in for supper. Unfortunately, she planned to eat them for supper. And so on.).

- As with all collaborative story-telling, the partnership currently being called on to come up with a scenario has to build on and continue the narrative cliffhanger that the partnership before them created. This does not work if children are trying to think of their contribution in advance rather than listening to the input that has come before.

My Shocking Secret

This is similar to the previous activity in that you display pictures of people on the interactive whiteboard.

The object is for the children, in partnerships or in groups, to come up with a shocking secret about that person that they wouldn't want other people to find out about (e.g. a sweet little old lady who poisoned her husband; a respectable-looking businessman who stole millions of pounds from a bank; a neatly turned-out schoolgirl who can read people's minds; a vicar who kidnaps cats that stray into his garden and keeps them locked in his shed).

This activity prompts the notion that people are not always what they might seem on the outside, and giving a character a secret they are desperate to conceal from other characters can add all sorts of interesting twists to an otherwise mundane story.

- Again, keep records of the discussions in a folder for children to access when stuck for ideas. It doesn't matter if they all 'borrow' the same character for a particular story; the important thing is that they use the character to develop the story in a direction that it wouldn't have taken otherwise.

Five Random Words

- Children each pick five words from a bag filled with 'fridge poetry' tiles (or make 'easier' versions of these for young children).

- Set the timer for ten or fifteen minutes, during which time they have to write a scene from a story including all five words they have picked.

  Reassure them that it's not quality of writing that they are aiming for – simply the task of getting all five words into the narrative practises associating random thoughts.

- It is a good exercise for the children if they see you having a go too (they need opportunities to witness you being a writer).

- Not having to write the whole story takes the pressure off, as does not having to start at the beginning.

Turning up the Heat

This is similar to the above, but this time, instead of events swinging from good to bad, they reinforce what the character is feeling in the first place.

For example:

Dan wakes up in a good mood, he hums to himself as he cleans his teeth. Mum has bought his favourite cereal for breakfast; he is pleased. There is an envelope on the table addressed to him. Opening it, he finds that his grandad has sent him a ticket for the big match on Saturday; he is delighted. At school, his favourite player is talking in assembly; Dan is excited. The famous star picks Dan to come onto the stage and demonstrate some moves with him; Dan is thrilled. As a reward, the player gives Dan a signed shirt and tells him that he and his grandad can watch the game from a VIP box on Saturday and meet the team afterwards; Dan is over the moon.

- Come up with a shared list of adjectives and get the children to fill in the blanks describing the events that lead from one state of being to the next.

Alternatively:

Ben wakes up feeling grumpy; it is raining and he has overslept. He doesn't have time for breakfast so pours a cup of tea, the milk is off and Ben throws it away in disgust. He runs down the street to see the bus disappearing around the corner; he is upset. He starts to jog to work, a car comes along and splashes him; he is angry. As he turns the corner, he accidentally bumps into a boy who is rude to him; Ben is furious. Stepping out of the way, he backs into the support for a shop canopy which empties a huge pool of water all over his head; now Ben is seething.

- You get the picture. Discuss feeling words and the order of intensity of their relationships (e.g. flat, fed up, disappointed, gutted, devastated; content, pleased, happy, overjoyed, elated).

25 Word Stories

This is an activity for older children where every word, literally, counts.

Writing a story in exactly 25 words (i.e. one or two sentences) that tells us – or more, likely, allows us to infer – a complete scenario, including motivation, backstory, emotion and viewpoint, is not an easy ask. But it is invaluable for practising the skill of 'less is more', for cutting back extraneous wordage with a surgeon's precision.

- Look online for examples of the genre – there are plenty as this form of 'flash-fiction' has captured the popular imagination. Or, for a real masterclass in concision, look no further than this gem by Ernest Hemingway in just six words: 'For sale, baby shoes, never worn.'

Character Point of View

What if we told the story of Cinderella from the point of view of the Ugly Sister (she might have something to say about being called ugly for a start), or from the point of view of the Prince or the Fairy Godmother?

What if, in the story of Jack and the Beanstalk, the giant was a lonely old (and off-puttingly large) man who felt misunderstood by the world in general?

What about poor old Dudley Dursley having to share his home and his parents with the uppity usurper, Harry? What if we gave these secondary characters a voice? What would the stories sound like then?

- This can either be a written exercise (with plenty of shared input to kick off the creative juices), or simply a hot-seating activity where the characters get a chance to put their side of the story.

Changing the Settings

Instead of focussing on the characters, what if some other aspect of a known story was different? How about setting Red Riding Hood in an urban housing estate, or The Princess and the Pea in a guesthouse in Clacton? Or on a spaceship?

Remember, this is not about generating swathes of evidence that the children can write. It's more to have a bit of fun playing with different scenarios that will, eventually, give the children confidence that they can come up with creative scenarios of their own.

This also works well with TV series. Consider a soap set on Mars, or under the sea, or at the South Pole. Who would the characters be? What would they do all day? Just being able to imagine the lives of people different from us is an essential skill for the story-writer.

- If the concept is too sophisticated for the children to run with independently (and it probably will be), just change one element and plan for the story (you don't have to write it) as a shared planning activity.

What If? Part Two

This time, we are going to play with a known story (either a generic one or a story that the class has read recently), and play with one of the plot elements.

What if, in the story of Cinderella, the glass slipper did fit on one of the ugly sister's feet? How would the story have gone then?

This is reinforcing the notion that all story events are either directly or indirectly linked to something else that happened previously (cause and effect).

- Again, the outcome does not have to be written. A joint plan and the conversation feeding into this are the effective ingredients of the medicine.

In the Middle of the Action

- Choose a passage from any point in a children's book (one page in length is about right). If it is in the middle of something happening or there is dialogue, so much the better.

- Read it out loud to the children and then set the timer for fifteen to twenty minutes. The challenge is to continue the story from the point it left off.

  It doesn't matter what the end of the story is going to look like or how it is going to get there; the children won't get to that part. The important thing is to continue the extract as seamlessly as possible, keeping the known details about situation and characters consistent (and, for better writers, keeping the style of the writing consistent with the original extract).

- You may have to support the children in asking themselves questions such as: who are the characters, and what are they doing?

Silent Movies

- When Eric Thompson wrote the English scripts for the 'Magic Roundabout' TV series in the 1960s and 70s (they were originally in French), he watched the shows with the volume turned down so that he had no idea what the original stories were, other than what he could infer from what was playing out on the screen. He then wrote his own stories to fit the action.

  Do the same with the children – show them a five-to-ten-minute clip of a movie with the volume turned to mute.

- After watching the clip, give out planning forms where the children can list characters (they will have to give them names at this point), identify the dilemma in the story and list the main events that they witnessed. Either you can leave it there (don't forget to put the plans in the writers' resource folders – someone might like to write this up during free writing time), or you can go ahead and set this as a writing task – to go on and write the story as the outcome for a long writing task.

- Older children can make notes on their whiteboards to remind them what they think is happening. For younger children, stop the film at regular intervals to discuss what you think is happening and scribe their thoughts for them.

Five Years Before / Ten Years Later

- Referring to a book that the children have recently read, invite them to create the backstory / future story of what happens to one of the characters (for example, at the end of the last Harry Potter book, J.K. Rowling tells us what happens to the characters when they are grown-up).

- Better pieces (or plans) will reference (or foreshadow) the events in the story we have read but even simple pieces should cross-reference character traits or physical description.

Write the Sequel

This is not unlike the above, but this time children are going to plan for the next episode of a known story. '...And they all lived happily ever after.' But did they?

What if Cinderella and the Prince had twelve cranky children and argued all the time?

What if the Prince lost all his money on a horse race and Cinderella had to go and work at a supermarket?

- Have fun with this one: the more outrageous the suggestions, the more the children will be engaged with the task. Keep the plans in writers' folders for reference later.

Missing Scenes from a Known Story

We all know the story of The Three Bears, but have you read the part where Daddy Bear phones social services to find out what to do with the small girl asleep in Baby Bear's bed?

Or the part in Sleeping Beauty where the Prince is riding through the forest to the castle and his hay fever is playing up?

Or any other 'extra' scene that you tell the children has been edited out of the book they have just read.

- Let the children discuss the possibilities afforded by the new instructions and then write the new scene collaboratively in pairs.

Genre Pages

- Begin by displaying, for example, a picture of a spooky house or graveyard (or the scene inside a futuristic spaceship; or a jungle explorer fighting off a big cat; or a Victorian urchin in a squalid-looking street; or a detective with a magnifying glass).

- Ask the children what sort of story this signals (in the same way that the illustration on the cover of a book gives the reader a clue as to what sort of book it will be). In the case of the house or graveyard, the children will probably tell you that it is a ghost or horror story.

- Next, discuss the features of this sort of story (mysterious and spooky happenings; ghosts, zombies, vampires and werewolves; general fear and sense of danger for the main characters; night time / midnight, etc.).

- Children then work in pairs to come up with a selection of choice words and phrases appropriate to this genre that they share with the class – you scribe the best ideas as they are presented on the board and around the original image.

- The final part of the exercise is for the class, as a shared activity, to compose the first few sentences for a story in this genre (or in the case of less competent writers, you model this part). Either the exercise ends there (with copies of the screenshot added to the writers' resource folders on the children's tables for use during free writing time – see below), or you can invite children to go on and write the story as the outcome for a long writing task.

- If this is part of a long writing session you can give extra time here for the children to check their ideas by scanning published books of this genre and adding to the list if they find other examples.

Filling in the Gaps

- Photocopy a double page from a graphic story and blank out the text.

- This exercise has two parts: firstly, in pairs, the children fill in the blanked text (probably dialogue) with their own suggestions for what is going on (this is in effect a story map or plan for the next part of the exercise).

- They then, individually, write the scene from the story based on this plan.

- Allow the children thirty to forty minutes maximum.

Opening Gambits

Present the following opening techniques and give them twenty minutes or so to write the start of a story

Start with Dialogue:

The story begins in the middle of a conversation. Ask the children to think about what the conversation is about; this needs to give the reader a clue as to what is going on (e.g. it might be obvious that the characters are packing up their things to move house or maybe they are having an argument in the car). From this the story gains momentum. If the characters are moving house, ask questions like: why are they moving? Where are they moving to? How do the characters feel about it? If they are arguing in the car, where are they going? What's the argument about? What does this show us about what is going on for each of the characters?

For younger children or less confident writers, give them the first couple of lines of dialogue and get them to continue from there.

- Sometimes it's easy to be enthusiastic about the initial flush of writing, but it's difficult to sustain over the long-term. So lower the bar about how much writing is to be produced: it doesn't matter whether the children go on to write the whole story, it's the experience of being in the flow for the moment that they need to embody.

Start with a Dilemma:

What if the first line of the story told the reader that the character was in the middle of being swallowed by a python? That would be a pretty good reason for reading on. Get the children to brainstorm a series of dilemmas that would just about guarantee a reader wanting to find out what happened next if this was set out in the first sentence of a story (these can be added to the writers' ideas box for free writing time). Children write the first sentence of their own story, which either tells us explicitly what the problem is or, for better writers, allows us to infer it. Share some of these and allow children to modify their own first choice if they choose, then set the timer for twenty minutes…

Start with an Ending:

- Give the children the end of a story where something dramatic happens, for example:

The sky gradually became darker as the approaching meteorite blocked out more and more of the sun. Abi reached out to Tom sitting in the deckchair next to her and gently squeezed his hand.

'I love you,' she whispered.

'I love you too,' Tom mouthed and the words, lost in the air, landed at the same time as the great chunk of rock hit the dome of St Paul's cathedral.

- Use this as a discussion tool for planning a story. Clearly there is probably no story after the events just described here, but there is a whole unexplored backstory that leads up to this scene. Who are Abi and Tom? What is their relationship? How long have they known about the meteorite? Have they had a part in trying to avert the disaster (or somehow caused it to happen in the first place – and if so, how)?

- Either do this as a shared planning exercise or get children to work with a partner to fill in the gaps. If they need support, give them a sheet with some open questions written on it to prompt their inquiring minds.

Start with a Description:

This is probably the hardest task because children's descriptions often revert back to the path of least resistance: a long and overblown account of what somewhere, something or someone looks like. Although we do want to know its physical properties, better pieces of writing allow the reader to make certain inferences based on the information provided.

For example, a description of a much-loved armchair might say it is:

'Overstuffed and as comfortable as a feather pillow, the fabric slightly worn down on the arms, a cosy tartan blanket draped over the tall winged back and a slightly tattered copy of the Radio Times waiting neatly on the seat to be called back into service at a moment's notice.'

Display a selection of images to jump-start the imagination, write for ten to fifteen minutes (you too!), then guide conversation along the lines of: who would own a chair like this? What is the most exciting thing that happened to them in the last week? What is the most important thing that ever happened in their life? Again, store the ideas for use later if wanted.

Opening Statements

Everybody knows dogs are the smartest creatures on the planet. Don't you just hate having a younger brother? Maths, ugh, the worst subject in the universe. Rainy days were invented so that mums could have a good old moan at you for bringing the mud in.

Statements or questions like these are a direct address from the narrator of the story to the reader, and as such they invite the reader's empathy, treating them as if they were a trusted friend or confidante.

Give the children a sweeping statement such as the ones above and ask questions like:
- Who would make a statement like this?
- What do their words tell us about them?
- What sort of situation might be typical for them?
- Where do they spend their time?
- What do they like doing? On the basis of this, begin…

- Allow fifteen minutes.
- Opening scenes and plans can be stored in writers' folders for continuing during free writing time if the children so wish.

Free Writing Time

Give the children an exercise book in which it is entirely up to them what they choose to write about. Either they can run with one of the exercises listed above where you have planned for a story but not actually written it, or they can write a scene for a different story or about something else altogether.

It's a good idea to have a box containing lots of cards with writing prompts written on them (e.g. write about a memory from when you were very young; or give titles or first lines to spark the children's interest). If they so choose, the children can go back to something they have already begun, either by extending it or by redrafting what is already there. It doesn't matter about the 'what' so long as they are engaged in writing something that catches their interest (they can even write a textbook about their favourite interest if this is what excites them).

These pieces of writing, although they are to be acknowledged by you and can be annotated with helpful suggestions about what they might try next, are not part of the children's formal writing output, and so they should not be assessed and should be marked with a 'light touch'.

- If your timetable allows (!), then it is a good habit to give the children say, thirty minutes in a week when they can write about anything they choose. If they are thinking of themselves as apprentice writers, they will constantly be adding to their writers' notebooks (word books) and adding to the writers' resource folders on their tables.

Chapter 4: Everything in its Place – Grammar and the National Curriculum

Learning the rules of grammar means being able to create sentences with words that follow the accepted structures of meaning-making and that are placed in the right order so that someone else can make sense of them. Grammar is largely divided into three main areas:

1. morphology – how individual words are constructed with the addition of prefixes, suffixes and inflected endings to base words to create a wider menu of nuances of meaning for those words

2. syntax – how strings of words are put together to form sentences

3. punctuation – the marks used to show the reader how to interpret chunks of text

The rules of morphology and syntax are common to both spoken and written language although spoken language sometimes allows liberties to be taken with syntax. This is why children run into difficulties when they try to write in the way they are used to speaking. Punctuation is a convention that is applied to written language only.

You already know the rules of grammar – you learnt them as a child when you began speaking. You would certainly be able to tell if the rules weren't being followed because the language, whether speaking or writing, simply wouldn't 'sound' correct.

However, knowing how grammar works and knowing how to talk about grammar are not the same thing. In order to talk about grammar we need a highly-specialised framework of vocabulary to verbalise our ideas and communicate them to other people. Being able to talk about language using a common terminology is essential for equipping children to discuss aspects of their own writing and, thereby, to maximise the chances of improving it. Conventions of morphology, punctuation and syntax are, after all, the niceties of writing that allow us to convey our intended meaning to the reader. Without attention to these finishing touches, the genius of our communication might never get through.

Indeed, in spite of any misperceptions that might have arisen from current preoccupations with testing of the subject in isolation, the real reason that we teach aspects of grammar and punctuation is to elevate the standard of children's writing. And the way to do this is through noticing grammatical choices in reading, and then talking about the author's intended effect of choosing exactly that construction, rather than any other, and using shared writing time to repeat the same conversations in relation to writing you are co-creating with the children. If they cannot apply the skills, there is little point in them being able to name parts of speech.

In practice, we have probably always taught these skills when teaching writing. It is just that now the focus is more prescribed. The bar that dictates what needs to be known has been substantially elevated, and the terms we use to talk about aspects of grammar need to be the same, no matter who is having the conversation.

Common language for discussing aspects of grammar is vital. If one teacher talks about 'speech marks', another talks about 'inverted commas', and a third refers to 'sixty-sixes and ninety-nines' to describe the same thing, there is bound to be confusion when a child moves from one class to another or sits a test.

Moreover, it would have been perfectly good practice in the past to present a particular aspect of grammar – embedded clauses separated by commas, for example – without ever actually explaining that this type of clause has a special name. Unfortunately, this not only disempowers children when it comes to the inevitable test-taking, it also deprives them of a vocabulary to refer to this type of construction when discussing their own writing efforts.

For this reason, the standardisation of terminology for discussing grammar as set out in the National Curriculum is very helpful. Children realise that the list of punctuation and grammar aspects to be mastered is probably shorter than they had been previously led to believe (as they are now only exposed to one way of describing each of them), and both teachers and children are equipped with an effective shorthand for discussing elements of sentence and text construction.

However, the reality for the moment is that we have to teach grammar not just for its application to children's writing, but also in order to pass tests. Let's consider each of those applications separately.

 The study of grammar has a point. If grammar is taught well, it helps – but only if we take on board that ever-so-critical clause: if it is taught well.
– *David Crystal*

Teaching Grammar in Relation to Writing

In theory, as we have discovered, this should not cover any aspects of grammar that have not always been implicitly taught when preparing children for their own writing. The difference now, however, is that children must be taught explicitly to speak the meta-language of grammar: knowing the correct terminology and how to apply it. And by definition, teachers must also be confident of their own ability here.

Although it is perfectly possible to prepare children to sit the test with formal deconstruction and numerous 'naming-of-parts' exercises, repeated studies have shown that this kind of learning has no impact on general writing standards. What we must do instead is use the opportunities presented during shared reading, drafting, redrafting and proof-reading to hone in on the micro-aspects of sentence construction, using the correct terminology (as a side-effect this will enhance their ability to pass the test). The objective of this is always to equip children with a menu of possibilities for playing with their written communication, rather than teaching them the 'correct' way to write a sentence.

The first thing you will need to establish is what exactly it is that a significant group of children in your class need to know next. Perhaps they have largely mastered the art of punctuating speech with inverted commas, but are careless with end punctuation. Or you may be in the position where you would love them to be using inverted commas in the first place.

One obvious place in the writing process where you could put your teaching efforts is during shared reading (an essential part of the writing process), in order to notice the purpose of speech punctuation and when real authors use it. Another chance is when creating a shared first draft: if purely modelling the skill, you would write the sentence with the punctuation you are hoping the children will replicate, and then invite them to notice what you have done. During shared writing with input from the children you might prompt them with questions such as: 'what punctuation do I need here?' or: 'is there anything missing?'

Another place where it would be entirely appropriate to bring the children's attention back to the mechanical skill of punctuation is before the children's final check of their own work (proof-reading). There is little point in them being instructed simply to 'check their work' without some kind of prompt as to the kinds of secretarial errors they are checking for.

The same general process also applies if you are investigating longer noun phrases, relative clauses, use of the continuous tense, or extending sentences using subordinating conjunctions. The only difference is that writing more of these would no longer be a proof-reading outcome; it would instead be a focus for redrafting in which we concern ourselves with the content of what has been written, rather than the mechanics of transcribing it.

What this means in practice is that you need to have a very firm grasp on which micro-aspects of writing you are using your shared writing time to promote. And also to have thought about the kinds of prompts and explanations that you will use with the class do this.

In Chapter Five you will find a more detailed explanation of how this process works: how to embed your grammar teaching into the body of the writing lesson in order to make it relevant and applicable to the task the children are currently undertaking.

Teaching to Pass the SPaG Test

As from summer 2016, all Year Two and Year Six children have been formally tested on the Spelling, Punctuation and Grammar elements of the National Curriculum. Explicit teaching of grammar in the body of the writing lesson as outlined above will go some way towards preparing them to be successful in the tests. Unfortunately, however, many of the pitfalls associated with being successful may not be to do with children understanding or applying the concept, so much as them being able to comprehend what the question is asking them to do (i.e. test-taking skills).

To this end, it is recommended that a discrete portion of the day (no more than five to ten minutes at any one sitting) is given to this test-taking element for pupils in Year Six (Year Twos will benefit from a lighter touch where a few exemplar questions are worked through as a shared activity in the week or so preceding the test). Practice tests should also be administered to establish where any confusion or weaknesses lie. Some detective work may then be required to determine whether these weaknesses constitute a lack of understanding of the concept, or whether the children were simply floored by the wording of the question.

If the problem lies in question interpretation (or being able to translate their correct verbal answer into an acceptable written format to gain the marks), then some practice in test-taking skills (modelled and guided practice leading to independent practice) is required. Use examples of other questions that rely on a similar wording and format for both question and answer. You should also use the framework of the original question that caused the difficulty to create new examples until the children are confident about answering these types of questions.

If the problem was that the children simply were not confident enough about the concept in the first place, another approach is needed. Although some elements of the tests rely on children being able to apply knowledge (essentially the same skill they are already using when applying concepts of grammar to their writing), a more likely stumbling block is that they are not used to analysing text for the purpose of classifying parts of speech (naming-of-parts). If this is the issue, some training in this is required.

A simple approach to this follows in the form of a week's cycle of instruction in one aspect of grammar classification:

1. Define the term
2. Classify
3. Deconstruct (identify)
4. Synthesise (apply)

For example, let us assume the children need some clarification of prepositions.

Day One

Define the term: A preposition is a word that shows how two parts of a clause are related. Explain that prepositions usually go before nouns, pronouns or noun phrases and show how these are related to another element of the clause or sentence. Give some examples, e.g.:

The cat is **under** the table.

Let's meet **before** Saturday.

Dan fell asleep **during** the talk.

I took the bus **into** town.

He gave the pencil **to** her.

At the end of the afternoon,

we went home.

(N.B. It is important that examples are given within the context of sentences because some words can have more than one function within a sentence, and that function will only become apparent when it is examined in context).

Explain that this combination of preposition plus noun, pronoun or noun phrase is called a **prepositional phrase**. It gives us information about how the two parts of the clause are related, and often tells us the position (in place or time), direction or relation of the following noun / pronoun to another noun, or to the action described. Very occasionally, prepositions can also precede adverbs or adjectives. (Also note that in the last example, the prepositional phrase also functions as an adverbial: it is not impossible for the same group of words to have more than one function in a sentence.)

Get the children to think of some more examples of prepositional phrases to add to the list and discuss, in each case, what sort of structure follows the actual preposition.

until now
over there
by far
in brief

Day Two

Revisit the definition and classification list if necessary, then get the children to identify the preposition(s) in a single sentence – choose the level of difficulty of the task appropriately – and tell them how many they are looking for.

Extend by getting the children to identify the **prepositional phrases** within the sentence.

The boy who was lying **on** the sofa called to his sister **across** the room to fetch him a glass **of** orange juice **before** he died **of** thirst.

The boy who was lying **on** the sofa called to his sister **across** the room to fetch him a glass **of** orange juice **before** he died **of** thirst.

Days Three and Four

Analyse a longer piece of text taken from a real book and with the children, pick out the prepositions / prepositional phrases. The key to success is to analyse the function of the words and phrases within the sentences to see whether this fits with what we already know about the function of prepositions and prepositional phrases. A useful part of the discussion will always be clarification of words and phrases if the children are unsure about whether they fulfil this function.

Day Five

Apply the skill (synthesise): get the children to fill in the blanks in the sentences below with an appropriate preposition / prepositional phrase for each:

The dog ran .... his owner.

Susie skated .... the ice.

Let's talk .... lunch.

Come and see me ....

None of the above mini-lessons should take longer than five to ten minutes per day (this is not a teaching point to be laboured as it is applicable to such a specific outcome). Nor should they constitute part of a writing lesson as they are not directly transferable to writing output. Instead, they should occupy a time-slot elsewhere in the day. Keeping the focus of the learning objective sharp and the pace of the teaching snappy, and reinforcing the children's understanding on a repeated basis, will be much more effective than a forty minute slot of grammar teaching once a week.

Another thing to beware of is that in many cases, a single word could potentially belong to more than one word class. We can only determine which type of word class it belongs to by examining its function within a sentence. For example, the words 'before', 'after', 'when', 'until' and 'since' could all either be prepositions or subordinating conjunctions. We need to see the word within the context of the sentence to tell which it is:

I won't have anything else to eat **before** lunch. (P)
We set off for Cornwall **before** the traffic got too busy. (SC)

Do not panic if this is confusing at first. We, as adults, are not traditionally used to analysing grammar in this amount of detail (it was off the curriculum for many of us who were educated in this country within the past fifty years or so). The main thing is to be confident about aspects that are already clear to us, and to refine our subject knowledge about those that might be less clear – either (if you are lucky) by having it the focus of a school training, or by investing in a good book. David Crystal's 'Discover Grammar' sets out the principles as clearly as any book that I know. It is also helpful if you have a 'study buddy' with whom you can clarify anything that seems particularly tricky.

Chapter 5: The Writing Toolkit – How to Make it Work Every Time

This is the nitty-gritty of the dilemma. It's all very well playing out fun and exciting writing scenarios in the format of imaginative games, but the point is that children often find it difficult to transcribe all their good ideas onto paper. They may have trouble writing at a consistently high standard for the duration of a sustained piece of text, remembering to pay attention to sentence structure, grammar constructions, punctuation, creative content, word choice, paragraphing, overall text organisation, spelling, handwriting, and other pesky pitfalls that ensnare the unsuspecting writer.

In this chapter, I have set out a series of steps that can be applied to writing anything, in any genre. It's a roadmap of sorts that the children can follow, knowing that by the end of the journey, they will have given the writing task in hand their best possible shot.

As I have stated, the children are apprentice writers. That means they must learn by looking over the shoulder of someone (you) who is already better-skilled in the craft than they are. It doesn't matter if you don't rate yourself as the next J.K. Rowling; the bottom line is that you will be more skilled at writing than the children you are teaching. This is all that matters.

It is therefore vitally important that you share the writing journey with the children. What this means in practice is: whatever it is that you are asking the children to write, you will need to give thought to writing a piece of your own that responds to the same prompt.

Years ago, when I worked as a consultant for a literacy programme that produced a lot of teaching materials, we began by writing all the first drafts that the teachers would share with the children, with the idea that they would pass these off as their own work. It soon became apparent that this was a terrible idea. With no ownership or investment in what was being shared, the teachers made heavy weather of the task, turning what should have been a creative and inspirational session into something mundane and mechanical. Not their fault, but they couldn't get excited about something they hadn't had a hand in creating. Worse, they couldn't begin to share their thinking processes about how each stage of the work had taken shape because they'd never been involved with its evolution.

In a nutshell, for each task that you set the children you will need to consider: what you will write about during shared writing time; which writer's thinking processes you particularly wish to share with the children; and what features of sentence structure, text organisation, punctuation, grammar, etc. you want the children to be practising.

You will also need to think about what, if any, support might you have to provide for some of the less able children in order for them to produce the same outcomes as their classmates. You will find more on differentiating and providing extra support in the next chapter.

The point of a writing process is that it is replicable. It doesn't matter what the children are writing about or at what level, they will apply the same process to its production. This way they will know that they have all bases covered in terms of text organisation, best creative content, best showcasing of that content in terms of how it is written, and attention to technical details like punctuation and spelling.

There are several models of writing processes out there, but they are broadly similar and I know from experience that this model works. Based on this, it should be straightforward to use the template provided to create your own lessons teaching any type of writing to any group of children.

The National Literacy Trust tell us that 'there is a clear relationship between writing attainment and enjoyment of writing – children who enjoy writing 'very much' are seven times more likely to write above the level expected for their age'. In contrast, children who claim not to enjoy writing 'at all' are nine times more likely to be writing below age-expected levels. Writing enjoyment and writing attainment are clearly interlinked: experience of one will lead directly to experience of the other. To this end, we must do everything in our power to set up writing opportunities that are presented as fun; to create opportunities to 'have a go' with a new skill, to try things out, to take risks in an environment that is non-threatening and supportive.

To make the learning environment as risk-averse as possible, you need to ensure that all children in the class are sitting with a writing buddy: another child writing at broadly the same level. You could also match them for having complementary skills, e.g. a child who has an active imagination paired with a child who is less imaginative but solid in technicality. This buddy will be their back-up support for testing and developing ideas, critiquing work and generally being available for reassurance and help when you are occupied on the other side of the room – which is, after all, most of the time.

Even young children can work well in this way as long as they have plenty of guidance beforehand on how they can best help each other. Resources such as dictionaries and thesauri should also be freely available on tables. On the other hand, if children get distracted by endlessly looking up bon mots in the thesaurus when they should be getting their ideas on the page, you might want to restrict provision of these to the redrafting process where the choice of the right word has become the point of the exercise.

1. What Will I Write About?

Sometimes, this part has already been done: we tell the children what to write about, no discussion (imagine the slipper did fit the ugly sister…; write a fact sheet about lions; write an information leaflet promoting Hogwarts School). But there are often times when the prompt is so general (write about a place that is special to you; write about a memory from childhood; write a ghost story), the pressure to come up with an idea – any idea – for the main topic of the writing becomes an almost insurmountable obstacle to writing anything at all.

For this reason, we need to reassure the children by sharing with them that all writers struggle to come up with the brilliant idea that will be the core of their next best-selling novel. Or they may have so many ideas that the problem is sifting out which is the best. Either way, the process is the same:

you talk through what is going on in your head when you are deciding what you will write about. This is a conversation that will be happening anyway; it's just that because you are already a proficient writer, you probably won't be conscious that you are having it.

Remember the process of learning to drive? While you are learning, you are acutely conscious of all the different things you have to do in order to set off for the first time: look in the mirror; signal; take off handbrake; depress accelerator, etc. This stage is called 'conscious competence', or even 'conscious incompetence' if you are really struggling with the whole thing.

Once you become proficient at driving, you no longer go through the mental checklist before pulling away; you just do it. This doesn't mean you are not performing the exact same range of actions as you were previously. It's just that you no longer need to keep the process in your conscious brain. This stage in the learning process is called 'unconscious competence': the stage where actions have become so automatic that we no longer need to think about them. This is where we are as fluent readers and writers. So the way to improve children's skills in both these areas is to unpack exactly what is going on for us, and to state our thought processes out loud as we approach each stage in the writing process.

Let's imagine I am getting my children to write about a time when they got into trouble for something. I am making the assumption that this will be in response to something in a similar vein that they have read, in which case, they will already have had a model for what a first-person recount looks like in terms of structure, style, voice etc. If this is not the case, then you might have to remind them how such a piece of text is set out, either in the form of a quick recap or by deconstructing another example of the genre.

Firstly, I need to come up with a range of options that I can choose from (and notice, the word 'I' here: it is vitally important that I am sharing my own experience of something that actually happened to me because I am talking through a process for selecting a topic for a recount of my own, not guiding the children to think about what they will be writing about at this stage).

I might come up with a few possibilities such as:

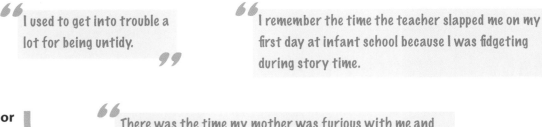

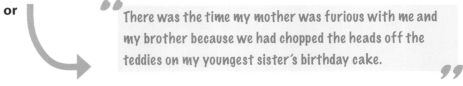

Once I've got a menu of possible topics to choose from, I need to select the one I'm actually going to use (remembering that the reasons for rejecting the other ideas are also valuable information for the children). I might decide along the lines of: 'I don't think I'm going to write about being untidy, it's not really very interesting and it was so common that I can't remember one occasion that stands out from the others. I could write about the teddy cake – that would make quite a good story. But I'm going to pick the story about my first day at school because that was a horrible thing to happen and I'm still upset about it all these years later.'

Once I have explained how I reached the decision for what I will write about, then it is time for the children to have the same conversation with their writing buddies. If they are not used to working like this, I may have to spend some time coaching them about what sorts of things they could ask their buddies in order to help them come up with ideas. This is also time that will give me a very satisfactory return on my initial investment as the children gradually become more skilled at facilitating their own writing processes and problem-solving at the point of need.

2. Test the Idea

The object of this part of the process is to test whether my chosen idea is going to work in practice: has it got 'legs'? Do I know enough about my subject? Can I tell the story of what happened? If I can tell a story aloud then the chances are I am also going to be able to tell it on the page. This part is the oral rehearsal for writing: talking through the story out loud to the children:

> It was my first day at infant school. It had been a horrible day, I'd missed lunch because no one had told me where to go. I was miserable and hungry. I don't remember what we'd done for the other lessons, but I do remember being happy it was story time at the end of the day.
>
> All the children sat on the carpet and Miss Peters was reading to us. I was enjoying the story and there must have been a little wooden toy train on the carpet next to me, I was pushing it backwards and forwards with my hand while I was listening – I don't remember actually doing that, I just remember the teacher saying: 'James, stop doing that!' Well, I wasn't James so, of course, I didn't really think I needed to take much notice – I just carried on doing what I was doing.
>
> The next thing I knew, the teacher had slapped me across the face and she was shouting at me. 'I told you to stop doing that!' Well, you can imagine how upset I was. It seemed so unfair. And that was my memory of my first ever day at school.

Notice in the above that I am not trying to craft beautiful sentence constructions or to be clever with my presentation. I am simply telling the story as I remember it. The crafting can come later when I'm actually involved with writing it. The purpose of this part of the process is to test both that I have enough to write about (i.e. the details to flesh out my story and make it interesting for the reader), and that the ideas flow coherently to the end, a huge stumbling block for most children.

Writing buddies then talk through their best ideas in the same way. My job at this point is to move around, helping to facilitate discussions by prompting the listening child to ask the right questions to tease more detail out of their partners, e.g.: 'tell me more about that bit – how were you feeling then?'

It may well be that this part of the process throws up the fact that I need to go and do some more research about the thing I'm writing about, or I might even need to ditch the first idea and pick another one. If this is the case, then I need to do that here. I won't go onto the next part of the process until I am satisfied that I can account for what I am going to write about by saying it out loud.

3. Story Road Map / Plan

Uh oh, planning! How many of us have children who, when we ask them to plan for a piece of writing, write out the first draft of their composition, complete with beautiful punctuation and handwriting? Not surprisingly, these same children are then a little put out when we ask them to write their first drafts – 'but we already did!' So, there are a few things that we need to remember about planning.

Firstly, that a plan is a working tool for the person who is doing the writing. Its function is to serve as an aide-memoire, so that when we are carried away in the delicious flow of getting all our thoughts onto the page, we do not forget to include any of the pertinent details we had previously gone to the trouble of thinking of, and we are clear at all times about the direction in which our writing is heading. Plans do not get marked, they are brief. They do not have merit in their own right and they are never, ever, an exercise in handwriting and presentation.

Probably the main task for this stage is 'un-teaching' the children to write in full sentences. Being able to record the main ideas for writing with just enough detail to flesh these out in the minimum number of words is the only requirement. So when I show how I record my own ideas for writing, I am focussing on note-making at speed and using just key words to represent ideas.

As long as I can understand what I meant by 'didn't mean me' in the outrageous case of mistaken identity as detailed above, then I am good to go. If the children still insist on writing in complete sentences, I won't give them time to – model writing just two or three words to record the main idea that I will write about, then set the board timer to thirty seconds so that the children can do the same. Then I repeat for my second main idea, and so on. In any case, the younger and less proficient the children, the more they will need this part of the process to be broken down and to be guided as they navigate their way through it.

Plans need to be written in a format appropriate to the finished piece of writing. I would not plan for something that has a linear flow (a story, a recipe, a newspaper recount, a historical recount, etc.) in the same way I would plan something that provides information or presents the case for an argument.

In the case of something that has a flow to the events (things that are either happening, or they did happen, or they might happen in the future), then it is appropriate to use a Story Road Map: a list of the main events with arrows showing how they link together.

This reinforces the cause and effect relationship between events – things happen because something else happened previously to set up the situation. Also, the map will need to be adapted to include details about who is in the story, where it is set (and, if appropriate, when it is set), and what is the main dilemma. The latter should be obvious from the events described, but it is making it more explicit for the children that stories need to have a dilemma, otherwise they are not very engaging for the reader.

Example Story Road Map – Shipwreck

Characters:

- Chris, Abi, Eli, Raj, Woof (the dog)

Setting:

- Tiny island – Caribbean – palm trees – sandy beach – blue sea – coconuts – scary insects and snakes
- Dawn

What happened:

- Day trip gone wrong – boat turned over by freak wave – washed on beach

First thing that goes wrong:

- Can't find Woof – drowned ?

Things get better when:

- Woof washes up on next beach – island seems live-able – fresh water, fish, coconuts – make shelter from palm leaves

Other problems:

- Snake in Eli's bed – A. hears 'ghost' in jungle – R. twists ankle, can't walk – fire won't light

Things can't get any worse when:

- Small boat– goes past (no fire)

In the end:

- Helicopters – children wave T shirts – rescued

Not all writing, however, is suited to Road Map-type planning. If I am capturing information (main ideas about a topic along with details that flesh out these ideas), then a traditional 'spidergram' plan is more useful. This suits planning informative pieces (non-chronological reports) and persuasive / discursive writing where the interest for the reader lies in the detail.

Example Spidergram – Dinosaurs

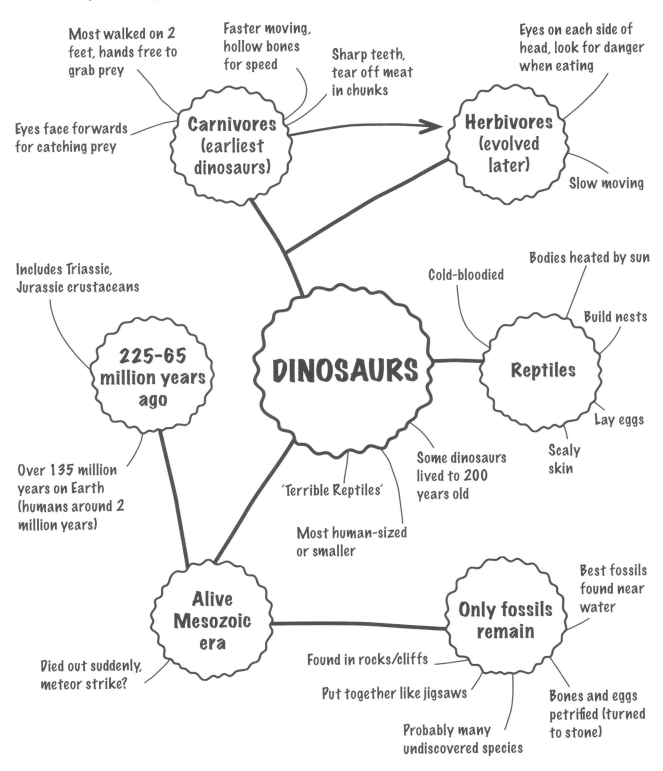

If you want to use photocopied skeletons of plans for the children to fill in their own ideas, this can be a useful resource if they would otherwise be overwhelmed by a blank page. But be careful with good writers that you are not limiting their thinking processes because you didn't provide enough boxes on the page to accommodate all the events they had planned for. In any case, we should be weaning children off pro-forma plans as soon as they can cope with blank-page planning, because this is a rehearsal for real-life writing.

 And a final word on the plan. Once committed to the page, unless you are a very competent writer (by competent, I mean a child who is writing at what used to be described as a level five or better), then on no account are you allowed to deviate from it (that is why it is called a road map). You can add in extra detail as it occurs to you, indeed, feel free to add in as much as you like. But you cannot leave the track altogether and start exploring new territory.

Lack of coherence in story-telling is one of the key inhibitors to children's writing progress. They need to know where their narrative is heading at all times. One of the key indicators that show the difference between a child who is beginning to exhibit competence in story-telling and one who is still on the first steps of the journey there, is that the first child writes stories that have an ending. They may still end in 'it was all a dream' but at least they end. The second group of children have no clue how to end their stories. They find themselves stuck on the journey, hurtling further and further from their destinations with no idea how to get themselves back on course.

In another life, when children's writing skills were externally assessed at the end of key stage two, it was my privilege to spend a lot of Junes marking these. I lost count of the times I would groan to myself in frustration when a story that started out quite promisingly reached its natural conclusion and then… carried on! A non-exciting but quite competent attempt at writing a story about something that happened at school might degenerate into incoherent ramblings as an alien spaceship appeared from nowhere and the passengers became embroiled in a brawl with some random characters from a TV series.

It was clear of course, from an objective viewpoint, what had happened. The child had got to the point in the story where they should have stopped, but there was time left for the task. The writer had looked around and seen their classmates still furiously composing and then panicked, writing more at the expense of the quality of the story (and probably losing the child a good level in the process). Instead of going back and making better what was already on the page, the child wrote more and killed the quality.

Again, it's a training exercise. We need to instil in children the confidence that when they get to the end of their plans, they stop. End of.

4. Get it on the Page

By this point, the children should be champing at the bit to get their precious ideas down on the page. They should practically be begging to begin writing – so confident are they about what they are going to write. If this is not the case, then it is probably a pointer that not enough time was spent on the previous three steps. You may be concerned about the amount of time the before-writing steps are taking, but this is good. It means you are probably spending just the right amount of time to prepare the children for being more independent later on. It is far better to begin with shorter pieces of confident writing created on the basis of high-quality discussion, than to have writing books filled with pages of rambling musings. Quantity we can work on later; quality is a non-negotiable at every stage.

This part of the process is the 'meat' of the task: getting the writing down in first draft format. Sometimes this is referred to as a 'sloppy first draft'. It's not that we are deliberately aiming for sloppy writing, far from it; but we have the reassurance of knowing we will get another sweep once the ideas are formed to come back and make the sentences sweeter.

It's important to instil in the children an understanding that this is not some kind of 'punishment' for not doing well enough the first time, it is simply the process by which all writers create work that is good enough to share with the world. And it is taking a natural pride in our creative efforts to want to polish them so that they shine as much as possible. If children seem unsure about the veracity of this, invite some well-known authors to come in and share their writing processes with the children.

The object of this part of the process is for the children to get as much as possible onto the page in the time that you set them to do it in. Again, you will need to make a judgement about how much time depending on how independent they are and how much stamina they have for long writing. If they do not score highly on either of these criteria, you will have to manage the time for them, telling when to write about the first event, next event… ending. Even if they are good independent writers, it is still a good idea to give a warning when the time is soon to be up so that the children can turn their minds to coherent endings.

As with every other stage, you will share the beginnings of your first draft with the class before they begin to write. Obviously, it is not good use of their time to watch you write out the whole thing, so a couple of sentences will suffice. And, if they are beginner writers, then a couple more sentences where you invite the input of their ideas while you scribe. It's essential here that you are clear about which skills you are sharing with the children – what exactly is it that you are teaching them to do?

If the children are very beginner writers then your focus will be on saying the sentences out loud before you write them to check that they make sense, and then labouring the point that sentences begin with a capital letter and end with a full stop. If the children are already good-ish writers then your focus might be on picking just the right sentence that is going to capture the imagination of your reader and entice them to read on.

In any case, this is where you deliver the requirements set out in the National Curriculum that relate to word, sentence, text-level and punctuation skills. You will teach the children these elements of grammar by talking about exactly how they work and then applying them to your writing. You will also be using the stated terminology to talk about them.

Now let's go back to the scenario about getting into trouble at school and consider how I might present this to my class of Year Threes. I am working on extending their range of sentence constructions by joining clauses together and introducing a wider range of conjunctions for them to choose from when doing so. I am going to remind them about inverted commas to punctuate direct speech when we get to the editing phase of the process, so for now I will concentrate on capital letters, full stops, question marks and exclamation marks, as well as reminding about apostrophes for contraction.

Me: I need to set the scene for the story so I'm going to write:

> (Writing) It was my first day at infant school.

Me: What shall I write next? I think I want to tell my readers what an awful day I'd had already because I want them to feel sorry for me.

> (Writing) It had been a horrible day.

Me: Hmm… I wonder if I could join those two sentences together? (Rubbing out full stop at end of first sentence.). What word could I put in here to join these ideas together? … Yes, if I put an 'and' in there then that sentence will make sense, now it says

> It was my first day at infant school and It had been a horrible day.

Me: Can we remember what kind of word 'and' is? … Yes, it's a conjunction because it joins two ideas or clauses together in a sentence. (Draw children's attention here to the fact that 'it' still starts with a capital 'I' – get them to tell you what is wrong with this now and correct accordingly.) I'm pleased with that sentence now, it tells us exactly what is going on at the start of my story. I wonder though, is it usual to have a horrible day on your first day of school? … No, not really, that's quite an unexpected thing to say (rubbing out full stop at end of sentence), I wonder if I can use a better punctuation mark than just a full stop to end my sentence that shows how unusual this would be? … (Add in exclamation mark in response to children's prompts.)

I then repeat a similar process for the second sentence (thinking aloud in the same way about the selection of extra words) until I have written:

> It was my first day at infant school and it had been a horrible day! I'd missed lunch and I was miserable and hungry.

If appropriate, you may also wish to use this part of the process to talk about the audience for a piece of writing (for example, if you were writing a story for a class of younger children it would sound quite different in terms of word choices, sentence construction and voice than if you were writing a formal letter of complaint) or about conventions of format if you were writing something specialised like a play or a letter.

Now, it's the children's turn to write. They are writing independently, but not necessarily in silence. If they need to check something with their writing buddy they should be encouraged to do this rather than sit and wait for your input every time they have a question.

My preference is that children write on every other line of the page. This is not essential, but in my mind it fosters the concept that we will be coming back to the page later to redraft. It's quite difficult – as well as quite dispiriting – to redraft something when we haven't got any room to make changes.

If the children are beginner writers, they should be encouraged to say each sentence aloud to themselves before committing it to the page. If they are more competent writers then they should be reading back to themselves every couple of sentences to check that what they have written makes sense and that the punctuation supports the meaning.

You need to give the children at least a ten-minute warning before the time is up so that they can reread what they have written and think about how to end their writing. They should know where the writing is heading because they have been checking the ideas against their plan – and ticking them off as they write – but they need to think about how they are going to manage this. It may well be that they also need some extra input at this stage about crafting endings.

If the children have only written a few sentences because they are very young, then you can go on and complete the rest of the process within the same lesson. But as a general rule, the writing lesson will stop here for today because we want the children to have a break from their writing so that they can come back to it with fresh eyes for the redrafting stage.

5. Review

The focus for today's lesson is going to be to up-level the quality of part of what was written yesterday. Children may find it quite hard to improve on their work without some kind of external input at this stage. So that input will come from two places: for some children, (different ones each session) from you and from the rest of the class as part of a group discussion; and then, for everyone, from their writing buddies.

What we want to remember here is that we are going to be up-levelling the content of what has been written (vocabulary choices, adding in extra detail, being more ambitious with sentence constructions, improving cohesion, etc.) rather than red-inking any miscellaneous commas or rogue apostrophes. Those will get their turn in the spotlight later.

Begin by giving the children a set amount of time to read through what they wrote yesterday. Even if they are perfectly able to read 'in their heads', encourage them to say the words very quietly to themselves as they read. This should highlight any clunky syntactical errors or gaps in cohesion that they might have missed if just skimming over the text. Even experienced writers see what they think they have written rather than what is actually on the page – this is why publishing houses employ proof-readers.

Once the children have re-familiarised themselves with their work they pick a paragraph or section that they would like to work on a bit more. This can either be because they are particularly pleased with it or because they feel that, somehow, it could just be that bit better if only they knew how.

At this point, ask for volunteers to share their work with the class. It's important that children feel confident to offer their work for group appraisal. If you have children who consistently do not want to do this, don't force them as they will still get the opportunity to have their work critiqued by their writing buddy, but try to encourage them to build up their confidence about offering work.

The writer then shares their chosen section by reading it out loud to the class (this way no-one is honing in on mechanical errors such as punctuation or spelling – these are not our chosen targets for improvement at this point).

The general rule is that the writer has then to hear two compliments about their writing before anyone offers any suggestions for improvement. Firstly, invite suggestions for improvement to the section as a whole (for example, 'you could use the pronoun 'he' sometimes rather than repeating the name 'Sam' quite so often'; or 'I liked the bit when Maisie went into the spooky house – could you tell me a bit more about what that was like for her?'). Then, guide the writer to select one or two sentences for further appraisal. Could a simple sentence be extended by joining two ideas together or by adding new ideas linked by co-ordinating and subordinating connectives? Could any of the vocabulary choices be improved by selecting a more interesting synonym or a word that gives a more precise picture of what is being described? Could any of the nouns be enhanced with the addition of extra details or could an adverb of intensity or frequency be used to give more precise information?

When one child's work has been discussed and suggestions offered for improvement, the author of the work thanks the rest of the class and, if time allows, another child offers their work for appraisal.

Don't spend too much time on the group discussion; the important part is to ensure that everybody gets a chance to discuss their writing with their writing buddy. Allow a reasonable amount of time for each child to read their work out loud to their buddy, and for the buddy to offer suggestions for improvement (but remind them about complimenting the work first). If the children are not used to working like this, then a significant part of your group discussion in the segment leading up to this will be focussed on training the children exactly how to give useful feedback.

When both children in the partnership have had their turn, they thank their buddies, recognising the fact that time to reflect and test work on a real audience is a vital part of the writing process. It gives us a chance to present our messages to the world in the most polished form possible.

6. Write-up!

This is the fun part. Here we are going to be polishing the rough gems of our ideas until they shine like diamonds (maybe even by adding some similes to our descriptions). Here we are going to be taking meticulous care that the content of what we wrote earlier has its chance to make its debut to the world supported by beautifully-crafted sentences and word choices. Nothing is random at this point: as writers, we take pride in our craft and we want our work to reflect this.

The children have already had feedback from their writing buddies – they don't have to implement the suggestions if they are confident about how else to improve their writing – but for children who may be struggling to know what to do next, some external input is another invaluable and reassuring source of guidance.

The first thing to note is that the children are not being expected to redraft the whole piece of writing (unless you have some real-life publishing objective such as a class newspaper, or a letter to parents that makes this an appropriate target). They are simply going to highlight one section or paragraph that they are going to finely polish in order to showcase their writing talent. If children can craft one section of their writing to a high standard, then the implication is that, given enough time, they would be able to do the same for all of it.

It is also worth noting that redrafting is NOT copying out in best handwriting. What happens when children copy out is that they do not make changes to the content of the writing, they simply replicate what was written before – or worse, they transpose mistakes into the redrafted version that didn't exist in the original copy.

This is where it helps if children have only written on every other line on the page – they can go back and insert, or change words, phrases and sentences without rendering the finished effort unreadable. It's important to reassure children here that neatness has its place, but what we are looking for, as an end result, is a piece of writing that looks like it has been worked on. This is what real writers do.

Just as before the first draft, you are going to use this time as a teaching opportunity for showing the children exactly how you improve your own writing. You can do this by considering more complex sentence structures; extending noun phrases; considering the exact vocabulary choice that matches the idea you want to communicate; adding stylistic techniques; and by the application of (not correction of – that comes later) more advanced punctuation choices.

Let's go back to our scenario of Year Three children writing about a time when they got into trouble. I will remind the children that, this week, we have been working on extending sentence constructions and that we do this by using conjunctions or 'joining' words to link our ideas. I am also, at this point, going to review the fact that direct speech needs to be contained within inverted commas. I will need to have a section of my own first draft to share on the whiteboard so that we can jointly redraft it (guided practice). To borrow a phrase from a popular children's TV series: 'here's one I made earlier'!

> I was listening to the story and pushed the train. The teacher said James don't do that. I carried on pushing the train. Then the teacher slapped me across the face she was shouting at me I told you to stop doing that.

Notice in the example above that I have not blinded the children with my dazzling writerly skills. Sometimes, as good writers – or at least better-than-the-children writers – it is easy to confound them by allowing no place to target their creative input because the writing was too good to begin with, so it is essential that I have left room for us to improve the writing together. Together, we redraft the writing, inviting suggestions from the children but very much guiding the sorts of input that might be helpful, until we might end up with something like this:

> I was listening to the story and **pushing the little wooden train at the same time. I wasn't really being naughty because I wasn't doing it on purpose. Miss Peters** said, "James don't do that," **but** I carried on pushing the train. **Suddenly she** slapped me across the face! "I told you to stop doing that!" she shouted.

In the above example, we have had plenty of chance to teach the objectives of the National Curriculum and apply them in context. We have created sentences with more than one clause and used a range of co-ordinating and subordinating conjunctions to link our ideas. We have used the continuous past tense to describe an action that was ongoing. We have added in extra detail to clarify the motivation of the narrator: viewpoint. We have extended a noun phrase. We have added in some prepositional phrases and adverbs that tell us about time. And we have used a pronoun to aid cohesion, a capital letter for a name, apostrophes for contraction, and inverted commas to contain direct speech.

Quite a lot of teaching input for a short piece of writing!

Now it's the children's turn. They should physically highlight the section they are going to work on with a highlighter pen (to stop them getting distracted by spreading the focus of their attention too thinly), and then apply everything we have just spoken about to improving their own writing.

They are not changing the story of what happened; just making the way it is presented more interesting and appealing for the reader. Now is the appropriate time to refer to thesauri to select just the right word for the job, and the occasion for the children to show off the full range of writing techniques they have learnt about. Less is more, as they say, but for now we'll settle for more is more until they become really skilled in the writer's craft.

7. Final Check

Up until now, we have been more concerned about the content of the writing, but now we must give some attention to the mechanics of it. Do the spelling, punctuation and general syntax support what I want to communicate or hinder it?

Allow the children some extra time here to give their work a final proof-read: checking that all the sentences make sense and have capital letters to begin with and end punctuation to finish with; that spellings are correct (use a dictionary if unsure); that tense choices are consistent; and that syntax is correct for standard English. If you feel the children need some input here in the form of a mini-session on commas to remove ambiguity, or the use of plural possessive apostrophes, this is where you can demonstrate the rules in context.

Because it is easier to spot mechanical errors in someone else's work than it is in your own, it is also a useful exercise to allow the children to cast their eyes over someone else's work (if they are mature enough) after they have proof-read their own. They can just hand the work over to their writing buddy, who skim-reads it this time rather than hearing it aloud. But it can be even more fun to get them to leave their open books on tables, then to stand up and mingle around the classroom for a set amount of time, before instructing them to sit and look at the nearest book. In either case, if someone else is editing the text for spelling and punctuation then they should use a different coloured pen so that you know this is another child's addition.

8. Take it to Press

On most occasions, the writing for this week is finished at the end of the previous stage. Nothing is likely to be added to the quality by copying out 'in best', and the danger is that the quality will actually be diminished if we are not careful.

But on some, very rare, occasions there is a real-life reason for taking the work to the next stage (publishing it). Perhaps you are preparing a wall display, or writing a class magazine that is going to be distributed to parents.

If you are going to do this, you will need to take the work away and mark it, giving final suggestions for improvement tweaks and picking up on spelling and punctuation errors that slipped through the net the first time round. Give time for word-processing or copying out the work and paying attention to the format but be warned – you will still have to allow for another proof-read when this is finished in case any errors were created in the transposition of the text.

After Writing Non-published Work

When children have just written in their books in the course of a normal writing lesson, then it eventually falls on you to go away and read what they have written. You will need to highlight sections worthy of specific praise (if they have successfully applied a skill that you were promoting during this lesson), and perhaps highlight one or two sentences (or words or phrases) as an invitation to improve them further. It helps to have two different coloured highlighter pens: one for 'well done!' and one for 'have another go at this bit'.

You should also signal if any punctuation is missing or if a common word is misspelt. For this to have any impact, you will need to allow children time, when you return the work, to read your comments and then make the changes you highlighted. It is better if this is a discrete ten minutes soon after completing the writing, rather than carrying it over to the beginning of the next writing lesson, by which time the children will probably have forgotten the flow of whatever they were writing previously.

When the children make changes to their work in response to marking, they should write in a different coloured pen from the one they used originally. This is done so that when books are used to make a judgement about progression and general quality of work, it is possible to separate the child's independent effort from what was done in response to your feedback.

One final word: children like consistency. They perform well if they know what is expected of them and how the outcomes will be judged. You may be a lone teacher with a mission to promote good writing in your particular class, or you may be part of a team effort dedicated to raising writing standards in your school. But if something works, it is worth sharing.

How much easier for children to transition from one class to another knowing already how things work and how things should be done. Results really improve in writing when it is taken on board as a whole-school priority and all teachers take on the same strategies to lift standards (albeit tailored to the differing abilities of the children).

Whole-school writing scrutiny where teachers see what children in other classes are producing can be eye-opening and informative. There is a lot to be learned from seeing where children start out in their writing journeys and where they are heading. As a side effect, this makes transparent things like presentation standards across the school and marking consistency. All good and valuable information for anyone working within the school.

The Writing Process – Outline of Stages

What will I Write About?
Generate broad ideas, decide on audience and format (if this has not already been set in the prompt)

Test the Idea
Talk through best ideas and choose one to write about

Story Road Map / Plan
Key words only to get the ideas on paper

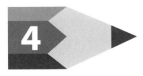
Get it on the Page
First draft – write as much as possible in the time available

Review
Self-assessment / peer-assessment – how could this be improved?

Write-up!
Up-level one section only – add extra detail / better vocabulary choices / more ambitious sentence constructions

Final Check
Check for spelling, punctuation and syntax errors

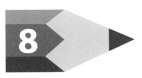
Take it to Press (optional)
Publish or make 'best' copy (remember to repeat Final Check stage if work has been copied out

Chapter 6: Scaffolding and Differentiation (use of writing frames and planning forms)

What would be the opposite situation to scaffolding a lesson? Imagine setting a writing task that begun and ended with the instructions 'I want you to write me a discursive essay about the pros and cons of children having to go to bed at eight o'clock on weekdays. You've got one hour – begin.' How many of your children do you think would stand a chance of even getting out of the starting blocks?

Scaffolding is the art of breaking down learning and learning tasks into manageable chunks – the size and content will vary to accommodate the children's developing skill repertoire – and providing tools, structures or strategies to make each chunk directly accessible and relevant. Differentiation is how you fine-tune the learning for the varying abilities of all the children in the group – this can either be in terms of the expected outcome (most commonly, the amount individual children are expected to write) or in terms of the level of support provided for individual children or groups of children to achieve the same outcome.

Effective scaffolding and differentiation have something in common. In order to meet children at the precise point in their learning development where they are currently operating, you need to know the exact distance between what children can do by themselves, individually and as a group, and the next learning that they can realistically be expected to achieve with effective assistance (the zone of proximal development). You will only know the answer to this with good formative assessment in place and up-to-date tracking documents that show you exactly what each child can and cannot do on the hierarchy of developing writing skills.

There are several general rules for scaffolding lessons. Always show the children the product they are expected to create (by giving text in the same genre for deconstruction prior to writing, and by modelling each stage of the writing process at a word, sentence or paragraph level – with a clear focus about what skills you are noticing or practising), before they are required to give attention to their own writing. Use think-alouds on an on-going basis that show children how good writers organise and problem-solve their writing tasks at every stage of the writing process. Give plenty of time for discussion at every stage. And review each stage with questions that test children's understanding of what they have just been learning as well as developing their ideas further (with flexibility to amend the lesson plan if there is a misunderstanding or lack of clarity at this point).

This is scaffolding based on the apprentice system, where the learner has a more experienced practitioner (you) to show them 'the ropes'. And it is something that is well covered if you follow the guidance for creating a consistent writing process in the previous chapter.

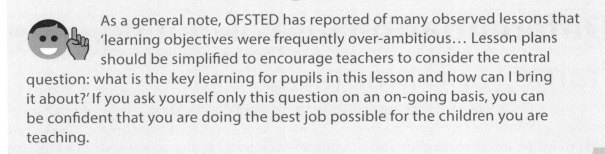

As a general note, OFSTED has reported of many observed lessons that 'learning objectives were frequently over-ambitious… Lesson plans should be simplified to encourage teachers to consider the central question: what is the key learning for pupils in this lesson and how can I bring it about?' If you ask yourself only this question on an on-going basis, you can be confident that you are doing the best job possible for the children you are teaching.

Using Props for Scaffolding

Scaffolding using props is a temporary support, similar to having stabilisers on a child's first bicycle. It is provided for just as long as it is necessary, and then gradually removed as the child begins to practise the skills independently. Tools that can be used either to scaffold the lesson for the whole class, or to give extra support to individual children or groups of children who need it, include the use of graphic organisers such as planning forms, story boards or writing frames; frontloading vocabulary that might be useful for a piece of writing (e.g. providing word walls or table lists of 'wow' words); using acronyms such as FANBOYS (the co-ordinating conjunctions 'for, and, nor, but, or, yet and so') or 'sentence bingo cards' to prompt children to create compound or complex sentences; and the use of pre-written text to practise redrafting or editing techniques.

Planning Forms

A planning form is a graphic organiser designed to help children record their ideas about what they are going to write about in a succinct and logical way, so that they have a record of their ideas to refer to once they begin to write. There are many ways of recording the ideas: a spidergram (or mind-map) is traditional, as is an idea tree where main ideas are developed with supporting details, or even a simple page divided into box-sections for the various ideas. It doesn't really matter how the children record their ideas, simply that they have an effective method for doing so that they can replicate whenever necessary.

A key rule for using planning forms is that children should write their ideas using the minimum number of key words only, written at speed (so not best handwriting practice) and specifically not in complete sentences. The latter is a vital skill to learn – and you may have to do much modelling to teach it – both in terms of getting their ideas down quickly (the skill of note-taking) and to prevent children from labouring over writing a complete story when you meant them only to plan it at this stage.

A planning form can either be presented to the children as a blank document or, if any of them need the additional support, as a partially completed document with ideas included that will spark off original thinking in the pupils. Examples of both follow.

Another rule is that mature writers should be encouraged to create their own plans on blank paper as soon as they are able to do this independently, so that they do not become limited by the constraints of the organiser you have put in front of them. And in order to maintain the coherence of the finished piece of writing, unless they are a very good writer, they will need to constantly refer to the plan when writing the first draft and not deviate from it (or write more once the ideas on the plan are exhausted).

Personally, I would not give beginner writers planning forms as it adds in a layer of mechanical complexity that they are not yet equipped to deal with (let them write straight onto writing frames with pre-written key words and phrases to introduce the next thing you want them to write about). In my experience, children become ready to begin to learn note-taking skills at around Year Three, but obviously there will be some element of individual maturity attached to this.

Example Blank Spidergram / Mind Map on Topic of Solar System

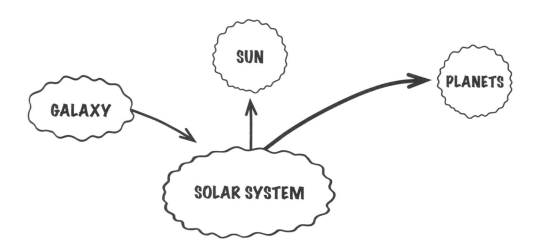

Example Partially-completed Spidergram / Mind Map on Topic of Solar System

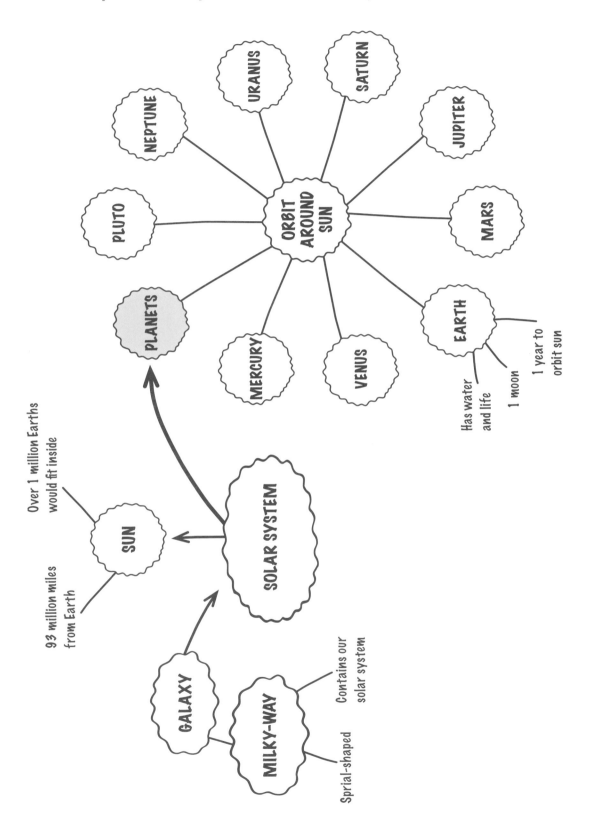

Example Blank Idea Tree on Topic of Aeroplanes

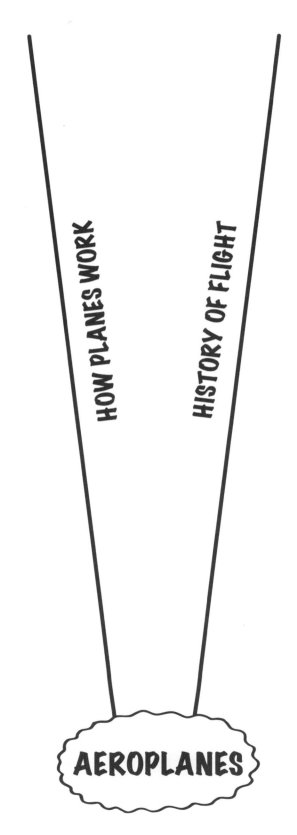

Example Partially-completed Idea Tree on Topic of Aeroplanes

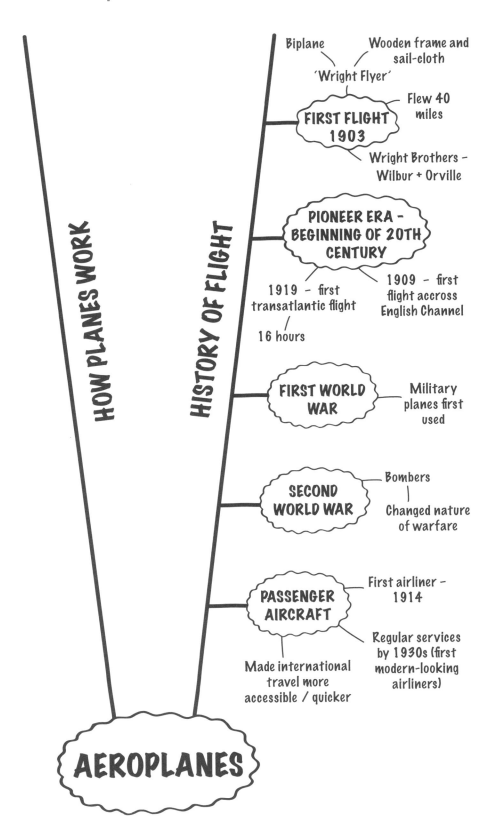

Biplane

Wooden frame and sail-cloth

'Wright Flyer'

FIRST FLIGHT 1903

Flew 40 miles

Wright Brothers – Wilbur + Orville

PIONEER ERA – BEGINNING OF 20TH CENTURY

1919 – first transatlantic flight

16 hours

1909 – first flight accross English Channel

FIRST WORLD WAR

Military planes first used

SECOND WORLD WAR

Bombers

Changed nature of warfare

PASSENGER AIRCRAFT

First airliner – 1914

Regular services by 1930s (first modern-looking airliners)

Made international travel more accessible / quicker

HOW PLANES WORK

HISTORY OF FLIGHT

AEROPLANES

Example Blank Planning Form for First-person Recount

Events	Thoughts and Feelings

What I learned:

Example Completed Planning Form for First-person Recount

Events	Thoughts and Feelings
My birthday – woke up	Excited Looking forward to fuss, presents, cake
Into Mum's room – no one there	Puzzled Weird
Checked Sal's room – fast asleep woke him - threw pillow	Cross! It's my birthday!
Heard Mum's car	Where's she been?
Mum got Taj from airport – big surprise!	Amazed, happy to see
Lovely day - cake Taj told stories about India	So happy Great to have Taj home Best birthday ever

What I learned:

People more important than things

Example Planning Form for Story (1)

Who is in my story?

Where is my story set?

What is it like there?

First...

Next...

Then...

In the end...

Who is in my story?

Sam
(a bit naughty)

Fred
(excitable - joker)

Jamie
(bit more cautious)

Where is my story set?

London zoo (school trip)

What is it like there?

Busy, noisy, lots to see

First...

In group with Miss Penny

Walking round, having fun seeing animals

Sam dares friends to slip off

Next...

No One notices – lose others

Lots of fun – being silly

Then...

Try to open lion cage – it's locked

Have a go at penguin enclosure – door opens

Spotted by zoo-keeper

In the end...

Zoo-keeper gets Miss Penny

Sent to sit on bus – everyone cross

Fred opens hoodie – penguin inside!

Example Planning Form for Story (2)

Characters

Setting

Story begins when...

First problem because...

Because of this...

Second problem because...

Gets worse when...

In the end...

Example Partially-completed Planning Form for Story (2)

Characters

 Ellie   Jack   Messy (dog)

Setting

Haunted house – old, dark, creepy, scary, falling-down

Story begins when...

Children go into house for dare - Messy outside

First problem because...

Door shuts – can't get out

Because of this...

Go further in – try to find other way out

Second problem because...

Jack's leg goes through floorboard – stuck!

Gets worse when...

Yellow eyes in dark – heavy breathing – scared

In the end...

Messy comes to see what is happening – passing hiker follows Messy in – worried something up – Jack rescued

Story Boards

A story board is a simple way of recording the development of a narrative using quick sketches to record events. This can be presented as a simple grid in which the children draw quick sketches to record their ideas. In the same way as for planning at speed, you will probably have to train them out of trying to produce their best art work as this is meant to be an aide-memoire for writing, not an end-product in itself. Tell them stick figures are more than fine for the purposes of this task.

Alternatively, for children who are just beginning their narrative-writing journey (and for older children who require more support), the story board can be presented with the story events already recorded. This removes the sometimes-paralysing dilemma of 'I don't know what to write about'.

Ready-made Story Board (1)

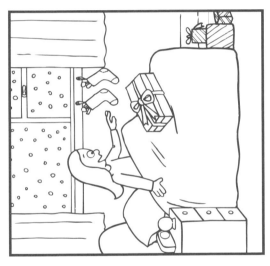

Ready-made Story Board (2)

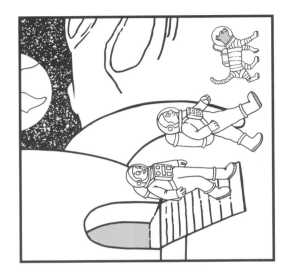
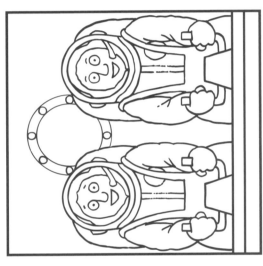
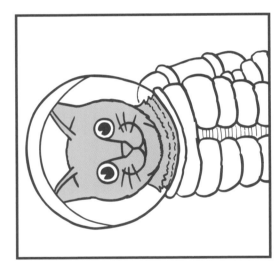

Vocabulary Lists

Frontloading the vocabulary that you are encouraging the children to use in a specific piece of writing is a good way of getting them to transfer words and phrases associated with various writing genres into their finished pieces. It also ensures they are familiar with any technical vocabulary they need to know to sound authoritative about their choice of subject matter.

The vocabulary can either be presented in the form of class 'word walls' if it is appropriate to share with the whole group, or in the form of 'table lists' if you are providing these only for some of the children in the group. Don't worry if all the children subsequently use the exact same vocabulary choices in their finished writing. As long as each child has applied the words appropriately, the finished product will be enhanced. Of course, if a child comes up with their own unique choice of pertinent vocabulary chosen for effect or precision, then this needs to be noted and praised accordingly.

Example Vocabulary Lists for Non-fiction Topics

Vocabulary for Topic about Spiders

- arachnid
- mandible
- fangs
- segmented legs
- thorax
- silk
- web
- prey
- paralyse
- liquefy

Vocabulary for Topic about Rainforest

- canopy
- forest floor
- flora
- fauna
- species
- endangered
- biodiversity
- camouflage
- remedies
- carbon dioxide
- oxygen
- indigenous
- pharmaceuticals

Vocabulary for Topic about Volcanoes

- crater
- lava
- magma
- ash
- vent
- erupt
- dormant
- extinct
- active
- gas cloud
- fault
- fissures
- mantle

Vocabulary for Topic about Knights

- chivalry
- honour
- jousting
- tournament
- steed
- spurs
- lance
- sword
- armour
- chainmail
- pennant
- favour
- squire
- coat of arms

Example Vocabulary Lists for Stories

Vocabulary for Traditional Tale

- once / once upon a time
- prince, princess
- king, queen
- castle
- tower
- kingdom
- crone, witch, woodcutter
- stepmother
- curse
- forest
- enchanted
- a hundred years
- riddle
- cottage
- gold

Vocabulary for Horror Story

- creeping / creaking
- haunted
- eerie
- overgrown / abandoned
- spooky
- ghost
- graveyard
- zombie / vampire
- forest
- goose bumps
- footsteps
- foggy
- midnight
- bats
- full moon
- werewolf
- howling
- omen
- foreboding

More Vocabulary Lists for Stories

Vocabulary for Pirate Adventure

- galleon
- ingots
- gangplank
- Jolly Roger
- captain
- bo'sun
- cabin boy
- deck
- ahoy
- anchor
- mainsail
- aye aye
- shiver-me-timbers
- land-ho
- attack
- crow's nest
- cutlass
- first mate
- treasure chest
- treasure map
- doubloon
- dagger
- parrot
- raid
- ransack

Vocabulary for Diving Adventure

- aqualung
- oxygen tank
- mask
- pressure
- valve
- mouthpiece
- bends
- wetsuit
- flippers / fins
- lines
- buddy
- shark
- barracuda
- cave
- octopus
- turtle
- clam
- coral
- clownfish
- angel fish

Aide-memoires for Developing Sentences - Sentence Bingo

By giving the children simple 'bingo' cards such as those that follow, then challenging them to tick the words once when they notice them in reading, and again when they use them in a piece of writing, they are by default creating a longer and more complex sentence than they might otherwise have done. With practice, using the bingo cards to remind them to create longer sentences, the children will eventually begin to write using more sophisticated structures independently.

Example Sentence Bingo 1 – Co-ordinating Conjunctions

and	but
so	or

Example Sentence Bingo 2 – Co-ordinating Conjunctions

but	nor
for	yet

Example Sentence Bingo 3 – Subordinating Conjunctions

because	after	if
when	although	until

Example Sentence Bingo 4 – Subordinating Conjunctions

unless	before	while	which
that	because	whether	although

Aide-memoires for Developing Paragraphs

Words and Phrases for Linking Events in a Story

- one day
- first of all
- once
- next
- then
- after that
- so
- that morning
- earlier in the day
- while this was happening
- meanwhile
- suddenly
- without warning
- as soon as
- at that moment
- during
- before long
- soon
- later
- in the afternoon
- that evening
- in the middle of the night
- an hour later
- the following day
- on Saturday
- a few weeks later
- at last
- eventually
- in the end

Words for Linking Ideas in an Argument

- firstly
- also
- in addition
- in fact
- what is more
- similarly
- however
- nevertheless
- on the other hand
- despite
- certainly
- usually
- undoubtedly
- controversially
- obviously
- naturally
- in general
- for example
- in other words
- to sum up
- in short
- finally

Writing Frames

A writing frame is a partially-completed piece of text (usually with just the sentence openers provided), designed to prompt the children to develop their own ideas whilst relieving them of the pressure to create a structure for their writing. Writing frames are particularly appropriate for beginner writers or older writers who have some kind of identified problem with the act of writing. Once children are able to plan sustained pieces of writing for themselves they should be able to dispense with the pro-forma frames as they will already have a structure for what they will write about.

In some cases, you may wish to add in conjunction words to encourage the children to develop longer and more complex sentences than they might otherwise have done (this is a good way of extending the challenge for more able beginner writers). Do not be tempted to provide more of the content than this, otherwise the exercise becomes simply a cloze exercise rather than a compositional writing task.

Once upon a time there was a princess called _____.

She was _____. Her mother

_____ and father _____

_____.

One day _____

_____.

Then _____

_____.

After that _____

_____.

In the end _____

_____.

Example Writing Frame (2) – Based on 'Not Now Bernard' by David McKee

In the Night

Bernard's mother turned off the light. _____

The monster _____

_____

_____

Next _____

Then _____

_____

_____

Example Writing Frame (3)

My greatest achievement is _____.

I think this because _____

_____.

Also, _____

_____.

Many people say that _____

but I _____.

I am also proud that _____

_____.

Now I know that I can _____

_____ and because of this _____

_____.

I think everyone should _____

_____

_____.

Differentiation

The reality is that it doesn't matter how streamlined the children's reading levels are within your class, you are always going to have a wide range of writing development to cater for. This could be manifested in writing stamina: how able are the children to apply themselves to longer pieces of writing and successfully control the structure of these? It could also be apparent in general skill level in handling language and a variety of sentence structures for effect. Or it could simply be the amount of support that children need in order to build a piece of text in the first place.

The first thing to remember is that, no matter where the children are on the developmental hierarchy, we are not going to be adjusting the objectives and outcomes of our lessons to accommodate individual children (apart from the expectation perhaps of how much each child is to write). Instead, we are going to be looking at how much support, or how little, the various children that we teach need, in order to achieve the same outcomes.

For example, I might have the objective of teaching the traditional tale genre to my children and have the intended outcome of them writing a story in the same genre, using traditional characters, stock openings and closings, a plot that involves a test of some sort, and applying the rule of three. Everyone is going to write the same story. The question is, what am I going to have to provide to various groups of children (or even to individuals if the need is high enough) in order for them all to be successful?

 Let us imagine that, in my class, I have a smallish group of high-flying children who are already demonstrating good imaginative story-telling skills and who do not particularly struggle with creating longer pieces of text (group one). Within this group I have a couple of children who I know will still benefit from a little hand-holding at the planning stage as they are slightly less confident about getting their ideas on the page. Group two, the majority of the class, still need a lot of guidance at each stage of the process along with a bank of resources of vocabulary choices related to the genre. Group three is a very small group of children who really struggle with managing the production of writing of any length, and expend a lot of effort on the mechanics of spelling and handwriting and make basic errors with their grammar and sentence structuring.

I will need to consider two things. Firstly, what kind of support in terms of props I need to make available to each sub-group of children in the class. And secondly, whether any individual children within those groups require even more tailored support than the rest of the group.

Writing a Traditional Tale – Extra Support Needed as Follows:

 Group One:

- Asha, Craig and Rhianna to plan on blank paper / blank planning forms for rest of group

- (Get children to create their own bank of vocabulary associated with traditional tales before beginning task)

 Group Two:

- Blank planning forms for Harry, Maisie, Prakesh, Ellie, Katie and Isobel / partially-competed planning forms for rest of group

- Vocabulary lists for words associated with traditional tales on tables

- Sentence Bingo cards on tables (but, for, because, when, if, that)

 Group Three:

- Planning forms – leave last two sections blank / completed story boards for Jake and Abdul

- Simplified vocabulary lists per partnership

- Word lists for partnerships – common spellings

- Writing frames for Jake, Abdul, Elliot and Saira

Remember that the point of providing the extra support listed above is so that the children will all produce the same output: a traditional tale according to the guidelines already set out. There will obviously be an additional expectation that the more-able children will write more than the ones who struggle at a more mechanical level, but essentially everyone is engaged in the same task.

This is important not only in terms of inclusion, but also because it keeps the bar of expectation high for all children, and not exclusively the ones who might, with little or no support, be predicted to clear it anyway.

There is an implication here in terms of preparation of support materials, but this will be more than compensated for during the delivery of the lessons. Your time there will be freed up to facilitate individual children's writing in a much more organic way, rather than being tied to support the same group of children because they don't have the creative and / or technical resources to complete the assigned task independently.

Chapter 7: But What about the Rest of the Time? (Quick solutions for giving attention to children's writing skills on a daily basis)

So far, we have looked at the process of supporting children to create sustained pieces of text that reflect their developing skills and stamina as apprentice writers. But the reality is that we are constrained by the demands of a curriculum. As it (rightly) requires that we expose children to the complexities of a wide variety of skillsets, perspectives on the world and knowledge bases, the opportunities for meaningful extended writing practice within one week may be limited (also see the next chapter for how to apply what we now know about good writing practice to other curriculum areas).

Yes, getting children to create one piece of extended writing each week covering a variety of genres will eventually be reflected in an increased confidence in the general process, as well as an increased ability to sustain and organise their thoughts. It will also, hopefully, manifest itself in a developing mastery of mechanical and secretarial skills. But in order to have real impact, we also need to be giving focussed attention on a daily basis to the act of selecting apt and precise vocabulary choices to convey nuances of meaning, and exercising our ability to create longer and more complex sentences.

Before I lose your attention and you place me firmly in the pile of 'nice idea but I don't have the time for this', let me state clearly that none of the activities I am suggesting in the menu that follows is meant to take more than five minutes (well, maybe one might take ten). Also, many of them are talk exercises, which means that children will not be obstructed or slowed down by their lack of secretarial abilities (the ability to physically form letters, spell words and punctuate sentences).

Everything we have discussed up to this point will, if implemented on a regular enough basis so that children become familiar with the routines, show as progression in their writing output. But this progress will be gradual as it relies to a certain extent on the children's own maturation both as readers and writers. In order to accelerate this process, wouldn't it be exciting if we could extricate those skills that are the hallmarks of good writers, but which also translate quickly into visible progress?

Let's consider what evidence we are looking for when we make judgements about whether or not a child is an accomplished writer. At the earliest stages we are looking to see whether they have the ability to translate sounds into recognisable graphemes on the page. Can they make plausible attempts at the complexities of spelling words in the English language? Do they have an innate ability to create a sentence that makes complete sense on its own; that reaches a logical conclusion before the next sentence begins (that does not spin off into a chain of cascading ideas loosely linked by words such as 'so' or 'and'); and, ideally, begins with a capital letter and ends with a full stop, question mark or exclamation mark?

If children are still mastering this stage of beginner writing, this is where teaching needs to be laser-focussed until they are competent in the art of writing recognisable sentences. There is no point in compounding errors at this fundamental level of communication by trying to introduce subtleties of the writing art that are frankly neither appropriate nor helpful at this stage.

Once children are equipped with the basic formula for creating longer pieces of writing (competency in forming and punctuating simple sentences), they can begin to string ideas together using appropriate linking words. They can gradually extend the amount that they write, start to consider word choices for special effect, and add in extra information about the things they are writing about. Here they are starting to have an awareness that their job as a writer is to interest the reader.

At this point, one of two quite interesting things often happen. Children may develop into competent mechanical writers (solid spelling and punctuation skills with good use of syntax and grammar), but their writing remains rather unexciting and 'safe'.

On the other hand they may develop into budding storytellers. Their writing could be chock-full of tension, drama or humour, and brimming with extra details to interest the reader. They could use exciting and adventurous vocabulary, express their thoughts using longer and more complex sentences and generally be creative and engaging to read. But then their overall performance is brought down by mechanical errors in syntax, punctuation and grammar that do not do justice to their general level of ability.

The key here is to determine into which camp a child falls and then to tailor support appropriately. The end goal is to train up writers who are both secretarially competent and interesting and creative, able to express their ideas in a way that is both appropriate and clear, and – where appropriate – entertaining for the reader. This is the benchmark of what we describe as 'secondary ready'.

The icing on the cake would then be to have a writer who is not only competent and creative, a proficient driver of the English language on the page, but also 'writerly'. A writerly writer has an acute sense of both their audience and the purpose for writing, and tailors their output accordingly. They use words and sentence structures selected according to the perceived preferences of the reader, and additional words such as adverbs to express subtle nuances of meaning. They are able to access a wide variety of vocabulary choices and sentence structures for effect, and the whole spectrum of punctuation to manage those sentence structures and communicate meaning precisely and efficiently.

This used to be classified as 'level five' writing. Not all children will scale these heights, and they will most certainly need to be avid readers before it can happen. But it is the level to which we are aspiring for all our children.

How do we get our children to reach this level of mastery? By paying attention to the details of writing on a persistent enough basis so that children become habituated in the thinking processes associated with an accomplished writer, even if they are not yet accomplished themselves.

This is a training process. We are literally rewiring the ways in which children start to think about constructing sentences, and introducing them to a variety of options for expressing their ideas depending on the effect they wish to achieve. We are teaching them to be discerning about language choices to convey an exact meaning, and to consider how the flow of their thoughts is presented in a way that is immediately accessible to the reader.

We do this by challenging them to express various ideas in different ways, and to consider what difference this makes to the fundamental meaning of the finished product. Do not worry at this point if this seems overly abstract.

What follows is a menu of options that you can present to children as quick five-minute 'fillers', ideally on a daily basis. These do not have to be part of any formal literacy hour structure. The impact will be created in the regular implementation of the activities (or 'opportunities for language play', since playing with words is what good writers do).

Your job is to analyse the children's current writing output to determine what it is that they need to know about next to move their writing on to the next level. This might involve considering their mastery of vocabulary; their ability to manipulate sentence structure to include all pertinent information and achieve a desired effect; and their ability to present their ideas in a cohesive and developmental way that makes logical sense to the reader.

It doesn't matter too much where the children are in their ability to commit ideas to paper. Most of the activities are discussion-based, which means that even if a child is unable to record the sentence on the page, he/she should be able to articulate it. And by constantly talking in ways that take account of how ideas are expressed, then by default, eventually, this will be reflected in the quality of children's written expression.

The only proviso I would issue here is when the children are not yet capable of writing in simple sentences that make sense on their own and begin and end with the appropriate punctuation. In this case, your attention should stay there until this basic structure of written communication is mastered. This is because everything else that we do builds on this ability and assumes that the foundation is already in place.

 Let's begin. Some of the ideas we talk about next will be appropriate for the level at which your children are currently writing, and some won't be (yet). But don't worry, the point is that this is a menu of activities: you get to pick and choose which ones you share with the children and which you save for later (or not at all). There is no hierarchy to the structures – you will need to apply your judgement about which ones will be useful for the children according to what is holding them back from being better writers than they are now.

Vocabulary – Using Language to Achieve a Precise Effect

If one element of writing could be considered worth its weight in diamonds when it came to assigning value to the various parts, it would be vocabulary: the word choices a writer makes in order to paint using the exact shade they have envisioned in their mind's eye. Telling us the lady took her dog for a walk in the park gives us factual information, but if each of us was asked to shut our eyes and conjure up the scene on our own mental 'cinema screens', then I would be very surprised if any of us were running the same movie. There are too many variables. Which lady? What kind of dog? Where is the park?

Consider the following sentences as alternatives:

The supermodel took her Chihuahua for a walk by the hotel pool.

Sergeant Holdsworth took her German Shepherd for a walk on the recreation ground.

The St Bernard took the maid for a walk on the common.

Okay, so I'm having fun with the last one, but you can see how it works. By being precise with our noun choices we leave no room for the reader to start playing a different movie from the one we intended. Remember, as authors, we are entirely in charge of what it is that our reader plays out in their head when they take in our words. And it is important not to allow too much room for variation. We don't want to surprise the reader with the information that our main character is a supermodel in the last act of our story when, in their mind's eye, they had already figured out that she was a train driver (unless, of course, manipulation of expectation is what the writer intended).

Activity – Precision Please!

1. Display a sentence on the whiteboard that deliberately contains generic noun choices, e.g.:

> The <u>woman</u> parked her <u>car</u> in the <u>car park</u> and pulled her <u>phone</u> out of her <u>bag</u>.

2. Ask the children what sort of word is underlined (they are nouns or 'naming' words). Discuss with the children the effect of the choices of these particular nouns (they are very vague – don't really give a detailed picture of what is happening). If the children struggle to see that these words are 'woolly' then invite them to shut their eyes and run the movie of what you are describing. Interrogate them afterwards as to what the car looked like, what the woman looked like, what kind of bag, what kind of phone, etc. They will probably be surprised at the variation of possibilities.

3. Invite the children, in partnerships, to select more precise choices for the underlined words. They don't have to write out the whole sentence, just make a note of the improved word choices. Then share some of these with the class to illustrate the new possibilities for the scene we have now set up.

 You could then discuss the possibilities for what might happen next in the various scenarios based on the new information we have been given. For example, the range of activities we might associate with a Skoda driver who pulls a 10-year-old Nokia out of a Tesco carrier bag might well differ from those of a Ferrari driver who pulls the latest model iPhone out of a Prada tote.

The following is in a similar vein, but instead of looking at noun choices, we are making verb choices for precision and meaning. This is a good tool for managing viewpoint in a story, where the difference between our character shuffling into a room, bursting into a room or sneaking into it makes all the difference to the motives and feelings we'd associate with their actions. This is particularly appropriate for replacing safe verb choices such as 'said', 'went' or 'put' with choices that more precisely communicate the character's feelings about what he is saying or about where he is going, etc.

Activity – Verbs with Vavavoom

1. Display a sentence on the whiteboard with a deliberately generic verb choice, e.g.:

   Dan put the wallet on the table.

2. Ask what kind of word the underlined word is (it is a verb or 'doing' word). Partners discuss other words that mean the same as 'put' but which have a more loaded meaning in that they give us clues about how Dan is feeling about putting the wallet on the table (Dan slammed the wallet on the table; he placed the wallet on the table; he slid it on the table, etc.).

3. Ask some of the partnerships to share some of their choices and lead a general discussion about how each of these alters the mood of what is happening, and possibly what might have happened to cause this in the first place.

 Remember that story action is built on a series of events that play out as a series of actions linked by cause and effect. Children add to their vocabulary books any words that are new to them.

No matter how you play with this one, the vitally important factor is that children are given access to a repertoire of exciting and adventurous vocabulary choices from which they can select the options that most precisely convey the meaning they intend. The best way to do this is to elevate the status of vocabulary, when you are reading and when you are talking.

As a minimum, children should have vocabulary books into which they are invited to record new words that appeal to them (a regularly updated class vocabulary board is also a good visual aid). Words can be 'borrowed' when met in reading, both when being read to – remember, part of your job is to discuss the effect of various word choices when reading to the children – and when the children are reading for themselves.

In the same way, it is helpful if you can be conscious of the vocabulary choices you use when talking to the children, perhaps choosing a word in advance that you would like to share with them and dropping it into the conversation. Adding new words to their vocabulary books is an ongoing activity that can be done at any point of the day: this constant vigilance for new ways of expressing ideas reinforces the children's identification of themselves as apprentice writers.

Activity – Word of the Day

Choose a word that the children wouldn't normally use in their everyday conversation, e.g.:

'partake', 'scrofulous', 'wizened'

The more unfamiliar it is, the more they are likely to remember it! The challenge is to drop the word as appropriately as possible, and as many times as possible, into everyday conversation – 'Shall we partake of lunch now?' 'Whose is this scrofulous old jumper?' 'My apple's looking a bit wizened, maybe I shouldn't eat it.' Points can be awarded every time a child manages to use the word of the day in an appropriate context.

A word about the organisation of vocabulary books: don't be tempted to organise them like mini-dictionaries with the words alphabetised. There would be very few occasions when a writer is seeking a word beginning with 't'. It is more useful to have the books organised in sections such as:

- Adjectives
- Powerful verbs (including sub-sections listing synonyms for 'said', 'went' and 'put' etc.)
- Opening phrases for sentences (usually adverbial phrases)
- Precision nouns (e.g. mansion/shack/cottage/apartment; Doberman/terrier/mutt/Alsatian; paperback/volume/album/scrapbook)
- Adverbs of frequency / intensity (sometimes/often/rarely/never; very/quite/so/somewhat/sort of/kind of/completely/wholeheartedly) etc.

Your guidance as to exactly what sections the books are divided into will depend on the level of the children's understanding of language structures. The point is that, ultimately, we are not seeking to have beautiful notebooks stuffed with interesting words and phrases (although this is part of the process). We are looking for those same interesting words and phrases to make it firstly into the repertoire of children's spoken vocabulary, and then also into their written work.

Your job as the teacher is to remind the children that they have these notebooks as resources to use while they are writing, and to reward them when a particularly apt or interesting word makes it onto the page. Just imagine, if children could collect new vocabulary words at a rate of one a day. That's five new words a week, sixty new words over a school term, and 180 new words over a school year. That's going to make an enormous difference in the long run to the quality of the children's written output.

Telling and Showing Sentences

'Show not tell'. That's the first thing any creative writing class tutor will tell their new students. Don't tell the reader what to think about the characters and events. It's much more interesting to let them form a viewpoint for themselves based on the evidence they are given. Consider the effect of each of the following sentences:

The giant squid was very scary.

The giant squid extended one of its enormous tentacles, dotted with saucer-sized suckers, over the glass side of the aquarium, and gently slithered it round the waist of the terrified curator.

OR

The baby was not very pretty.

I tried hard to admire the baby, but try as I might, I could think of nothing kind to say about its screwed-up, bawling face that resembled nothing so much as a currant bun.

Yes, there is still space in writing for simple sentences that just tell us what to think – if they are consciously placed in a body of writing for that effect. But, as a general rule, the second sentence for each of the examples would be considered 'better efforts' by the children. The first example explains exactly why the squid is scary and the second lets the reader work out for themselves that maybe the baby isn't the most appealing representative of its kind. From a reader's perspective, the extra details provided in the expanded versions of the information are better value.

A simple rule of thumb for teaching showing sentences is to eliminate words such as 'is', 'was' or 'were' followed by an adjective from descriptive passages. Rather than telling us that something is terrifying, boring, irritating or excruciating, tell us what is happening and describe how the characters are reacting to the situation. Instead of telling us that a character is sinister, uptight, lazy or intelligent, tell us what they might be doing to suggest these traits. Describing the movie that is playing in intricate detail allows us to reach these conclusions for ourselves and it's a much more engaging process for the reader than being spoon-fed the information.

Even beginner writers can play with telling and showing sentences. A sentence is compact enough to be committed to memory, and it is not necessary to write the improved versions on every occasion. Practising composing detailed showing sentences as an oral activity is a rehearsal in the long run for writing.

Activity – Show not Tell

1. Write a 'telling sentence' on the board, e.g.:

> Miss Cruncher was a very strict teacher.
> The cat was enormously fat.
> The cake was a masterpiece.

2. Challenge the children, in partnerships, to come up with a showing sentence that leads us to the same conclusions as the original sentences, but without stating the words '**strict**', '**fat**' or '**masterpiece**'.

3. Share some of the children's new sentences and, if appropriate, elaborate on them further with input from the rest of the class.

This can be great fun: the madder or more outrageous the examples, the more creative the children will be with their revisions and the more they will enjoy the task.

Don't worry if the children are not actually writing their sentences most of the time. Just practising this activity on a regular basis will ensure that, eventually, the children will begin to approach their writing in the same way at the point of composing sentences. This is also a good opportunity for guided redrafting when marking children's work: highlight a sentence that the child has written with an invitation to upgrade it to a showing sentence.

Building Noun Phrases (Including Extra Information to Interest the Reader)

Most children will already know that a noun is a naming word: the name of a thing or of a person or of a place, etc. A noun phrase is simply all the words (including the noun itself) that tell us about the thing (or person or place) that we are writing about. For example:

- A cat
- A black cat
- A friendly black cat
- A friendly black cat with a diamond collar
- A friendly black cat with a diamond collar and yellow eyes
- A friendly black cat with a diamond collar and yellow eyes which was rubbing itself against my legs
- A friendly black cat with a diamond collar and yellow eyes which was rubbing itself against my legs and purring loudly
- A friendly black cat with a diamond collar and yellow eyes, the most beautiful of creatures, which was rubbing itself against my legs and purring loudly

All the above examples (except the first, which is simply a noun) are examples of noun phrases. Don't let the children be thrown by the number of words contained within the phrase. If it relates to the noun and gives extra information about it (and does not make sense on its own, i.e. it still needs a verb to complete the sentence), then it is a noun phrase.

The extra details we include about the things we write about are the jewels that make our writing sparkle. The fact that the last example also contains embedded information (contained within the commas), and a clause introduced by a relative pronoun (which), are cherries on the cake. These can be dissected and discussed with the children if they are ready for this level of analysis (it is a helpful tool for reminding them to replicate these features in their own writing).

If they are not ready, you can simply play the game of how much more information can we give about the thing we are writing about, without concerning them with the technical terms. Good writers generally write intuitively. They may know, if pressed, how to deconstruct the elements of their sentences, but they do not generally construct them in such a formulaic way. They simply write in a way that is rich with detail.

Activity – Building up the Brushstrokes (1)

1. Display a picture on the whiteboard that shows the thing you want the children to describe.

- For lower levels it can simply be a picture of, for example, a house, a person, an animal, or a place.

- For higher levels, have something going on in the picture that can also be included in the extra information about the thing we are describing (in the example above the cat would be rubbing against someone's legs rather than just sitting there).

2. The first child names the thing we are describing (the noun).

3. The second child tells us something extra about the thing we are describing (the most simple way to do this is to add an adjective), and the third adds another detail (this could be another adjective or a relative clause).

4. The next child adds more detail, either to the part(s) of the phrase that exists so far, or by adding another part to it.

 It is important that each child says the whole phrase created so far including their new information about it. If you wish, you can write the new information as it is offered, but this is not necessary – the point of the exercise is to add as much detail about the noun as possible without actually completing a sentence about it.

Activity – Building up the Brushstrokes (2)

A more sophisticated version of the above activity is to challenge the children to extend the information contained within the noun phrase from their imaginations, i.e. without the picture on the whiteboard to prompt ideas.

This is a skill that directly relates to the craft of storytelling: the ability to make up details about places, characters and situations that did not previously exist outside of the writer's imagination. The only proviso is that extra information offered should not contradict the viewpoint that the earlier details have already started to paint of the subject.

If, for example, we have already described a cat as being friendly, we cannot then include the information that its sharp teeth glistened menacingly, as this would detract from the cohesiveness of the statement (we will cover the skill of maintaining consistent viewpoint later).

You may well get to a point, if the children are skilled at this activity, where so much extra information is included about the noun that the phrase becomes unwieldy – i.e. there is too much information in it. This does not matter. The fun lies in seeing how much you can say about the subject without including a finite verb that would complete the sentence (the moment we say 'the black cat sat on the mat' rather than 'the black cat, which was sitting on the mat', we leave nowhere for the information to expand).

'Less is more' is a more complicated concept than 'more is more', and for the most part we will be pleased for the children to err on the side of generosity when including descriptive information about the things they are writing about.

A more focussed way of targeting the kind of insertion that you want is to show where you want the extra information:

Activity – Fill in the Gaps

1. Provide a sentence that includes a certain amount of information about a noun, but to which more information can be inserted in the form of a relative clause or an embedded clause.

2. Challenge the children to come up with the extra information required (show where in the sentence it is to go – i.e. do you want a selection of adjectives or an embedded or relative clause?), then compare results.

For example:

The car chugged up the motorway at precisely forty miles per hour.

The funny little car chugged up the motorway at precisely forty miles per hour.

The funny little car chugged up the motorway at precisely forty miles per hour.

The funny little car, driven by four clowns, chugged up the motorway at precisely forty miles per hour.

The funny little car, which was belching smoke alarmingly, chugged up the motorway at precisely forty miles per hour.

The funny little car that I had spotted earlier at the service station chugged up the motorway at precisely forty miles per hour.

This activity is continued on the next page. ⟶

Or

Alan Grimswald stared at the strange animal in utter disbelief.

Alan Grimswald, the famous TV naturalist, stared at the strange animal in utter disbelief.

Alan Grimswald, who had spent his entire life searching for the yeti of the Himalayas, stared at the strange animal in utter disbelief.

Alan Grimswald, whose sense of humour seemed for once to have deserted him, stared at the strange animal in utter disbelief.

Different Types of Sentences

1. Simple, Compound and Complex Sentences

A sentence needs to make sense and to stand alone as a complete unit of information. At its very simplest, it will contain a subject and a verb. Convention teaches us that it is also demarcated with a capital letter to signal its beginning and a full stop to signal that it has ended.

Simple sentences can also contain extra information about the subject (noun phrases) or about the verb (adverbs), or a prepositional phrase (tells us where, when or how), but they still only have one verb that tells us what is happening in the sentence.

- The mouse squeaked.
- A tap dripped.
- The wind howled.
- Abigail whispered.

- The little brown mouse squeaked.
- A tap, somewhere in the building, dripped annoyingly loudly.
- The wild wind blowing icily from the North howled.
- Abigail whispered cautiously into the phone.

Often, simple sentences contain an object as well as a subject (a 'do-ee' as well as a 'do-er'):

- The dog bit **the postman's leg.**
- Mr Plumtree wrote **a letter.**
- I saw **Grandma.**
- Alice ate **a sandwich.**

Again, we can add extra information about any parts of these sentences, but they remain simple because there is only one main action being described (one main clause):

- The vicious dog bit the poor postman's leg for the third time that month.
- A furious Mr Plumtree wrote a letter of complaint to the council.
- I saw Grandma on the platform waiting for me.
- Alice ate a chicken sandwich with great gusto.

 Note: in the example above, 'waiting' is not a main verb – it does not constitute a part of a sentence that makes sense as a stand-alone unit. A simple sentence is usually short (but it does not have to be). Its defining feature is that only one main thing happens in it.

Once we can write a sentence in which one main thing happens we can begin to compose sentences in which more than one thing happens (compound or complex sentences). The difference between a compound sentence and a complex sentence is that in a compound sentence, the two actions are of equal importance:

- I will go to the supermarket and I will buy some vegetables for the soup.
- I could wear my trainers or I could wear my boots.
- I might read my book this afternoon but I might not have time.
- Tom fed the dog then he took it for a walk.

In a complex sentence, one of the clauses depends on the other in order to make sense (it is subordinate to it):

- **Although Sam had had a sore throat earlier in the day,** his performance in the concert that evening was a huge success.

- I think you will be a famous writer one day **because you can tell a story so convincingly.**

- **When you can talk to me politely,** then I will listen to what you have to say.

The clauses (parts of the sentences describing the various actions) in both compound and complex sentences are joined by conjunctions. In a compound sentence these are called co-ordinating conjunctions ('and', 'but', 'or', and 'so' are the most common), and in a complex sentence they are called subordinating conjunctions ('because', 'when', 'although', 'unless', 'until', 'if', 'since', 'despite', 'so that', etc.). If the subordinate clause comes at the beginning of the sentence, it is separated from the main clause by a comma.

Children generally learn to write in short simple sentences. Then they progress to longer simple sentences and compound sentences joined with words like 'and' or 'then', and on to more complicated structures by beginning to use words such as 'because' or 'when'. Being able to use a variety of interesting connecting words is a necessary step on the journey to creating more sophisticated sentence structures.

Activity – Conjunction Conundrum

1. Write sentences on the whiteboard that contain more than one clause (either compound or complex), but with the connecting word that joins the clauses missing.

2. You can either provide a bank of words for the children to choose from, or challenge them to find their own that complete the sentences in a way that makes sense.

 When children encounter a connecting word that is new to them, they can add it to their vocabulary books. .

Activity – Sentence Bingo

1. Challenge the children to spot conjunction words (words that connect clauses within sentences) as they read.

2. Make bingo cards for tables or partnerships that have these words written on them (ones you would like the children to use in their writing).

3. As the children find the words again in reading, they can cross off the words on their bingo cards. The winner (of part one of the game) is the table or partnership that crosses off all the words on the bingo card first.

4. The next part of the game involves the children crossing off the same words (either give new bingo cards or get them to cross off in a different colour) when they write their own compositions. In order to have used all the words on the bingo card, the children will have had no choice but to compose compound or complex sentences.

 The children have written in more complicated sentence structures than they might otherwise have done. And eventually the 'training' will pay off in that the children will start to use these words in their writing without the incentive of completing the bingo cards.

The reason that we need to be able to write using a variety of sentence constructions is that we will then have various shades available to us in our writer's paintbox. Sometimes, short, simple sentences have a useful function. They introduce the topic of a new paragraph; give a sense of pace or urgency to writing; add contrast for effect; and refocus the reader when used following a particularly long or complex sentence.

Long, complex sentences are useful for providing us with all the information needed, including details, nuances, references or explanations. They can also slow the pace of a piece of writing or create a mood of laziness and relaxation. Skilled writers use a variety of sentence constructions for interest and effect, and know that they are doing this.

In reality, what often happens is that children stop at the point that they learn to write complex sentences and neglect to vary the diet by re-introducing simple sentences for effect. This has to be a consciously taught transition, and the way to do this is through analysing sentence structure in other writers' work.

Activity – Sentence Forensics

1. Enlarge a passage from something you are reading as a class and display it on the whiteboard.

2. For each sentence, determine whether it is simple, compound or complex.

 Remember that just because a sentence has a lot of words in it, that doesn't necessarily mean that it is complex. Highlight each sentence to show what kind of sentence it is then go back and discuss the effect of using each sentence type where it was found.

Activity – Ring the Changes

1. Either use a passage you have written that relies solely on either simple or complex sentences, or use a real example that a child has written. Pitch it at the level the majority of children are writing at.

2. Display the passage on the whiteboard and redraft as a group exercise to include the missing sentence types so that the resulting piece is more varied and interesting to read.

3. Children then apply the same skill by redrafting a section of their own work.

 Develop a marking policy that the children understand as a shorthand for explicit invitations for improvement, for example, highlighting in a certain colour could mean 'can you make this sentence longer or more interesting by including a subordinating conjunction?

Activity – Keep the Sentence Going

This is a quick-fire activity in which the children take turns to contribute just one word to a sentence that still leaves room for the next person to add to it. No child wants to be the one to 'shut the sentence down' or to complete it.

1. Child one says a word to open a sentence (e.g. 'once', 'the', 'one'), child two contributes a word that is supported by the first word ('once upon', 'the first', 'one day'), child three adds another word ('once upon a', 'the first time', 'one day when'), and so on.

2. Each child must say the whole sentence composed so far with their word added to the end.

 Children will learn that the trick is to listen carefully to what has gone before – not to try to think of their word ahead of time – until they know the whole sentence starter that they are being fed. They cannot know in advance what kind of word is needed from them. In this way, children will learn what kinds of words extend sentences, and what kinds of words complete them.

It is important to share with the children that you are not practising creating extremely extended sentences because this is necessarily an example of good writing. You are practising these kinds of sentences because you are learning how not to shut sentences down when there is an opportunity of extending them (and because it is fun).

2. Statements, Questions, Exclamations and Fragmented Sentences

These are yet more shades available for the writer's paintbox so that we can compose with more subtlety and achieve a greater range of effects in our writing.

Questions are useful for creating realistic dialogue, or manipulating mood in dialogue. They can be addressed directly to the reader to give a sense of intimacy and engagement with the writing (as if they were engaged in a conversation with the writer), or can be rhetorical (requiring no answer but intended to give the reader 'pause for thought').

Exclamations add fear, excitement or a sense of surprise (Aaagh! Oh!), emphasise the unexpected quality of a situation (His face had turned bright green!), or generally add emphasis to an argument (This is wrong! Take action now!).

Fragmented sentences are sentences that are incomplete: they do not stand alone or make sense by themselves according to the rules of grammar. The difference between these and just poor writing is that the children know how to write in complete sentences; they have just chosen not to here. They are often exclamations as discussed above (Aaagh!) or sentences that begin and then trail off (But… I thought you said…). They are useful for adding realism to dialogue or can be used to give a feeling of the reader being engaged in a conversation with the writer. It is only appropriate for children to use this type of sentence in their own writing when we know that it is a conscious choice – not a result of being unskilled in the art of sentence construction.

Again, the way to mastery is for children to analyse other people's writing before beginning to apply the skills to their own writing.

Activity – Sentence Forensics

As before, choose something representative of the genre you wish to emulate and analyse it, sentence by sentence, discussing the effect of the selected sentence types.

It is worth noting that certain genres, e.g. persuasive writing, make much use of rhetorical questions or exclamations to promote a sense of urgency and rally the reader to action. Analysing dialogue to see how it differs from narrative writing is a good step on the road to mastering the art of characterisation.

Sentence Openers

One way in which we achieve variety in our writing (along with using a variety of vocabulary and sentence constructions) is to open our sentences in different ways. The most common way of constructing a sentence is to begin with the subject and a verb:

- The school was certainly an unusual one.

- Caitlin is my best friend.

- This cake is delicious.

- Patrick won the chess tournament for the fourth time in a row.

Even complex sentences, when we analyse them, often begin in the same way unless we make conscious choices to vary them:

- **Samantha turned off the light at 9 o'clock because she didn't want to get into trouble.**

- **We can go to the beach tomorrow unless anyone has any better ideas.**

- **Miranda sadly went back to the restaurant where the tragedy of the previous evening had played itself out.**

- **Mr Harding counted the children carefully when they got back on the bus in case anyone had been left behind.**

However, if this is the only way we begin our sentences, our writing will soon become repetitive and uninteresting for the reader. Analyse stories you are reading as a class and examples of genres that you wish to replicate in writing (e.g. newspaper reports, persuasive writing, discursive writing, information writing) to see how accomplished writers vary their sentence openers. Encourage the children to collect any clauses or phrases that particularly catch their fancy to add to their vocabulary books.

What follows is a selection of different challenges for children to practise playing with their sentence construction. Nothing need be written down; this is just as powerful when practised as a talk activity with partners. The key is to talk about (and play with) sentence construction frequently so that the children eventually take this process into their writing composition.

Activity – Reverse the Clauses

Challenge the children to begin a sentence with a dependent adverbial clause.

> As you are so certain this is the right way, I'm going to let you take charge now.
>
> Unless anyone objects, let's eat our sandwiches as we talk.
>
> Because Marco is afraid of the dark, he likes to sleep with the door open.

 If this feels too difficult as a completely abstract activity, supply the children either with the opening clause and let them finish the sentence (or supply them with the main clause and let them find the opener that relates to it) or simply supply them with the subordinating conjunction that will begin the clause (see Appendix 2 for a list of these).

Activity – Where, When, How or Why

Similar to the above, but this time the children will begin the sentence with an adverbial phrase rather than a clause (the difference between a phrase and a clause is that a phrase does not contain a subject and a main verb). Adverbial phrases are often prepositional phrases acting as adverbs and they tell us about where, when, how or why something happens.

> Back in the lab, the scientists were trying to work out what had gone so wrong with the experiment.
>
> During lunch, Tabitha announced that she was now a vegetarian.
>
> Without the slightest hesitation, Dan stripped off his clothes and dived into the freezing water.
>
> In order to look different from her sister, Jools cut off all her hair with the kitchen scissors.

 Provide the main clause and challenge children to provide the where, when, how or why that precedes it.

Activity – Unhappy and Afraid

Sentences that begin with a pair of emotive adjectives catch the reader's attention because we want to know what has happened to cause this state of affairs, or what the character might do next as a result of this.

> Unhappy and afraid, he wished he had never begun the journey in the first place.
>
> Furious and humiliated, Sam told Naomi that he hadn't wanted to be in the stupid play anyway.
>
> Exhausted and tearful, Rayah pulled off her sandals and dipped her feet into the cool water.

 Provide a linked pair of emotive adjectives and challenge the children to finish the sentence.

Activity – Start with an Adverb

Children are usually quite familiar with the adverbs that end in –ly that modify a verb:

> Happily, I can report that the operation was a success.
>
> Ashamedly, Herbert explained to the others that he had lost all of their money.
>
> Desperately, Hannah tried to convince the others that opening the door of the tiger's cage might be a bad idea.

 You might need to remind them of examples of adverbs that do not take the –ly ending (remember they will usually give an indication of time, of frequency, of place, of intensity etc.

One day, when you are older, you might remember what I have said.

Sometimes, in the early evening when the birds were singing just so, Clara remembered the night of the ball.

Upstairs, the children were making a camp out of the duvets and having a party all of their own.

Very well, that is your decision and I must respect it even though I think it will lead to trouble.

Provide a list of these sorts of adverbs (see Appendix 4) and display them as a poster to remind children to use them in their writing.

 Occasionally, pick one example randomly from the list and challenge the children to imagine the sentence that might follow it.

Activity – Begin with the Action

Starting the sentence with a participle phrase (ending –ing), puts the reader directly in the middle of the action – a useful trick for a writer who wants to draw their reader into a story.

Stirring his coffee with a fork, Dad complained yet again that something in this house was eating all the teaspoons.

Blowing a huge bubble out of the car window, Tabitha told her mum that she didn't care what people thought.

Trembling, Julian backed slowly away from the crocodile.

 Give the first part of the scenario and allow the children to have fun imagining the second part.

Activity – Past Participle Phrases Acting as Adjectives

Sometimes, it is useful to describe what something is like by describing what has happened to it:

> Clogged with leaves, the drain started to overflow.
>
> Eaten by mosquitoes, we realised that pitching our tent by the lagoon had not been the most sensible plan.
>
> Stuck in the toilet, Amelia wondered how long it would take for anyone to notice that she was missing.

 As above, provide the first part of the scenario and allow the children to make up the second part.

Activity – How to…

A noun clause is a clause that takes the place of a noun. Often it can begin with the words 'how to'.

> How to get out of tidying his room was Nick's most constant pre-occupation.
>
> How to teach the dog to speak English was a puzzle that Sean was currently working on.

 Brainstorm with the children some examples of noun clauses beginning 'how to' and then play with ideas about what might run on from these sentence starters.

Activity – What…

Another noun clause could begin with the word 'what'.

What you see is what you get.

What Megan had to say surprised everyone.

What happened next was completely unexpected.

 Brainstorm with the children some examples of noun clauses beginning with the word 'what' and then play with these to create sentences.

Activity – The Fact That…

One particular type of noun clause begins with 'the fact that…' This is a more informal way of stating information than beginning a sentence with 'that'.

The fact that Peter was a genius had not gone un-noticed in his family.

The fact that the sun had failed to rise that morning was creating a lot of concern in the village.

The fact that I had grown antlers in the night was something I was struggling to disguise when I went down to breakfast.

 Give children sticky notes to fill out as partnerships. Together they complete the clause beginning 'The fact that'… Collect in the sticky notes and post them on a notice board.

Partners select another sticky note to complete the sentence (or you assign them at random).

Activity – A Perfect Child (Appositive Phrases)

An appositive phrase is a noun phrase that renames another noun right next to it.

> A perfect child, Florence never once answered her mother back or argued with her brother.
>
> The disgusting armour-plated creature, a cockroach, scuttled across the table towards my cereal.
>
> An absolute disaster, the day had been destined to go wrong right from the moment I woke.

Give the children the noun you want them to rename and get them to confer with their partners to come up with an alternative phrase to describe it.

After that, they can construct the rest of the sentence in the way modelled above.

Activity – Absolute Phrases

An absolute phrase contains a noun and a past participle:

> His life's work completed, the professor wondered whether he should take up fishing.
>
> The washing hung out, Mum took ten minutes to have a nice cup of tea.
>
> The words said, Lenora turned and stalked away, her chin held high.

Provide the sentence starter and get the children to come up with the sentence that follows.

Activity – Whew! (Not Strictly a Sentence Starter!)

Introducing a sentence with an exclamation or interjection can add variety and excitement to a piece of writing.

'Whew! That was a close call,' gulped Ben, wiping the sweat from his forehead.

'Aaaaaagh! What do you think you're doing, letting Sid slither around the living room like that?'

'No! You cannot be serious!'

Make a poster of interjections that children might include in their dialogue and brainstorm situations where they might be appropriately used (the point being that the sentence that follows needs to link directly to the interjection).

Strictly speaking the examples above constitute more than one sentence, but they're still fun to try out and can add humour and spark to writing that might otherwise struggle to get off the ground.

Coherence and Cohesion

The coherence of a piece of writing describes how well it hangs together as a whole: does it have a distinct beginning, a middle section that develops the ideas and adds detail and interest, and an ending that wraps everything up tidily? Cohesion refers to how well the various parts of the writing hang together: do the paragraphs or sections relate to one another, presenting ideas in a smooth flow? And do the sentences within a paragraph relate to one another, referring backwards and forwards with ease and grace?

Tackling coherence is – by its nature, since it is a whole-composition judgement – not a quick fix that we can necessarily address here. The only way to get better at this skill is to have repeated and frequent opportunities to practise extended writing. Cohesion, on the other hand, is something we can practise in bite-sized chunks.

One of the easiest ways to achieve a cohesive effect in writing is to use nouns and pronouns appropriately. Generally speaking, the first time we introduce something in a piece of writing or the first time we refer to it in a paragraph, we will use its proper name (Michael, the house, Grandma). Thereafter it is perfectly acceptable to use a pronoun to refer to it (he, it, she). As we used the proper name earlier in the paragraph, it can be expected that the reader will know who or what it is that we are talking about. Early writers often fall down because they use the name of the object or person repeatedly (Michael went to the shops. Michael bought some apples. Michael put them in his bag.), or they forget to introduce the subject of the sentences completely (He went to the shops. He bought some apples. He put them in his bag.). Achieving a balance so that they neither confuse nor bore their readers is a skill that children need to master early on in their writing journeys.

 Activity – Proper Pronouns

Display a short passage that you have prepared on the whiteboard where the subject of the sentences is named repeatedly. For example:

> When it was noon, Gretel shared her bread with Hansel, who had scattered his on the path. Then the children fell asleep and evening passed, but no one came to help the children.

> The children did not wake until it was the middle of the night, and Gretel was afraid. Hansel said, "Just wait, Gretel, until the moon comes up, and then we shall see the crumbs which I have scattered on the path. The crumbs will show us the way home."

> When the moon came up the children set off, but the children couldn't see any crumbs because the birds had eaten all the crumbs. Hansel said to Gretel, "Don't worry, we shall soon find the way."

> But the children did not find the way. The children walked the whole night and the next day too, but the children did not get out of the forest and were very hungry, for the children had nothing to eat but a few berries which were growing there. And at last, the children felt so tired that they could go no further and the children lay down beneath a tree and fell asleep.

Alternatively use a child's actual piece of writing for redrafting. If this is a trap that they fall into, they will not mind their work being used for this purpose. Collectively, analyse the writing to establish what is wrong with it (repetition of nouns) and highlight where these should be replaced by pronouns. Make the changes according to the children's suggestions.

 A variation of this is to write the piece so that it is made confusing by over-use of pronouns and then make improvements to it in collaboration with the children. (Since you are not rewriting the whole piece, this still meets the criterion of being a five-minute exercise.)

An extension of the above skill is to use different ways of referring back to the same thing in order to give variation to the writing (Michael, he, the boy, the youngster). Start by analysing examples in books you are currently reading together (or write something expressly for the purpose of analysis) and noting the various ways that the writer refers back.

Activity – Naming of Parts

1. Display a passage that uses various references to the same thing for the children to analyse. For example:

> Nick pressed himself against the rock as the giant fish lunged towards him missing his breathing tube by inches and skimmed past into the dark water. Seconds later, he braced himself a second time as he saw the shark reappear and turn to face him. It appeared to look at him directly and then gathered speed in the same instant to attack again. Nick shut his eyes and prayed for the end to come quickly. He felt the whoosh of water as the monster was on him and then, nothing...

2. With the children, highlight the various ways in which, in this example, the shark is referred to (the giant fish, the shark, it, the monster) and discuss the effect of using these words rather than just 'the shark'.

 The exercise can be extended by including a continuation of the same passage, in which the references to the same noun have been blanked out and the children contribute their ideas for words and phrases to be inserted.

The above exercises encourage the children to think about how their writing flows: how does a writer hold a thought and refer back to it in a way that is both clear for the reader and non-repetitive?

Transitional Words

Transitional words and phrases are words that are used to 'glue the ideas together' in a piece of writing: they might link a paragraph to the one that precedes it, or link a sentence to the previous one. Such words are signposts, signalling whether an idea is about to be developed and expanded upon, whether it is about to be contradicted, or whether something completely new is about to be added to the equation. For the same reason that we use pronouns in our writing, such words help the ideas to flow in a way that is both clear and pleasing to the reader.

Examples of such words might tell us:

- about the sequence of ideas (firstly, secondly, finally)
- that an additional point is to be made (furthermore, also, again)
- that an illustration or example is to follow (for example, to illustrate, for instance)
- that a comparison or contrast is to be offered (in the same way, however, on the other hand)
- that an idea is to be clarified (i.e., to explain, to put it another way)
- about the timing of events in a story (then, meanwhile, earlier)
- about the place where the action is happening (nearby, far away, there)
- about cause and effect (since, because, as a result)

It is useful for children to have a bank of these words and phrases (i.e. collect them in their vocabulary books) as they form a helpful scaffolding for constructing extended pieces of writing.

Activity – Moving On

1. Display a (short) passage from a story or another genre of writing that you are currently working on replicating and analyse it to identify the transitional words and phrases.

2. Discuss the effect these have on making the ideas hang together in a way that is logical and easy to follow.

3. As a second activity, display another passage (same genre) with the transitional words and phrases blanked out. Children work together to decide which words or phrases best fill the gaps.

 You might find it useful to have a poster of such words and phrases displayed for this activity so that the children have a bank of vocabulary to try out for 'best fit'.

Remember that the activities suggested above are only five-minute 'fillers'; do not try to deconstruct a long passage here that would take much longer to discuss. The effectiveness of the exercise lies in reminding the children on a frequent basis to watch out for such 'tools of the trade' and to use them in their own writing. They only have to practise the skill in small bursts for this to become part of their automatic thinking-about-writing behaviour.

Viewpoint

Viewpoint guides the reader as to how they should be feeling about the ideas or events that are being described. This is most obviously apparent in a piece of persuasive writing where the writer tends to be very explicit about how they want their reader to think and feel about a particular issue. All writing has some element of viewpoint (whether it is the viewpoint of the writer themselves about their subject matter, or of the various characters that have been created within a story world), but more subtle pieces will be less obvious about the ways in which they manipulate the reader's emotions. Wherever they are on the journey to being able to convey viewpoint implicitly, children need to know that viewpoint needs to remain consistent, whether it is the writer's own view being expressed or the various viewpoints of different characters.

 Activity – Change of Mood

1. Display a passage such as the one below that conjures up a definite mood for the reader.

Scott sensed the alien before he could see it and a strange high-pitched sound that came from nowhere drilled into his head. He felt it getting closer now, a sense of imminent terror that sat in his stomach like a stone and the creeping chill of its body as it neared his hiding place. He imagined that he heard its long, slow breath, felt it extend a deadly tentacle towards the doorway in which he was cowering.

2. Discuss with the children what kind of mood is being created here and then highlight the individual words and phrases that support this.

 As an extension activity, discuss the possibilities for this not being a scary piece but describing an encounter with some other kind of creature (a friendly dog or a frightened rabbit). Redraft the identified words and phrases to support the new viewpoint. In order to bring this in under the five-minute limit, you could assign individual sentences to different children.

The important point to convey in the above exercise is that we are not necessarily attempting to improve the writing, but simply to play with the word choices to see what sorts of different effects we can create.

Another aspect of viewpoint is the skill of characterisation: being able to create characters who have defining features and can be identified by the consistency of the way they are presented, either through their behaviour or by their manner of speaking.

Activity – Says Who? (1)

Display a short piece of dialogue from something you are reading as a class but with the names of the characters who are speaking removed.

Challenge the children to identify who is speaking on the basis of what they are saying / how they speak.

Activity – Says Who? (2)

1. Using something you are reading as a class, make up several statements that different characters might say or think based on what you know of their viewpoint of the story events.

2. Children have to decide who would have made each statement.

Extend this by challenging the children to think up some more examples of things the various characters might say.

Paragraphs with Punch

This is the only activity in this chapter that will take ten minutes rather than five. This is because it is not possible for the children to hold several sentences in their heads at the same time; they will need to do this as a written exercise (writing as a partnership on a whiteboard is a practical way to do this).

If the children do not have the manipulative skills to compose a whole paragraph in a reasonable amount of time, you can also do this activity as a shared writing exercise where you write in response to the children's suggestions. The only other proviso is that the children will need to have a solid grasp of telling and showing sentences before they move onto applying the skill.

Activity – Paragraphs with Punch (1)

 1. Display a paragraph that you have composed that is structured in the following way:

- Telling sentence that gives you an idea of the subject of the paragraph
- Two showing sentences that develop this same idea
- A telling sentence that recaps the main idea to finish

For example:

> Viking warriors were probably not too hygienic. They tended to have long beards and hair that would have been unkempt and more than likely full of food debris. Also, it would have been difficult to wash their clothes often as they did not have washing machines and it is unlikely that they would have had a lot of time to fit in baths and showers while they were out conquering new territories. It is possible that you might have smelt a Viking approaching before you saw him.

Or:

> Dolores was not feeling at her best that morning. When she looked in the mirror she saw that there was a huge pimple in the middle of her forehead and her nose seemed to be alarmingly red. She tried smiling at the reflection but only succeeded in alarming herself. Entering the beauty contest was a really bad idea she thought to herself.

 2. Get the children to analyse the writing, sentence by sentence, to determine whether it is a telling or a showing sentence. Challenge them to come up with the formula for writing a paragraph set out above.

Being able to give the children a formula for constructing a paragraph was for me something of an 'aha moment': I knew intuitively how to construct a paragraph myself, but always found it a frustratingly abstract concept to share with the children. It's interesting to start analysing paragraph construction in this way and it seems to work for any genre. In a piece of persuasive writing, for instance, the showing sentences will develop the argument set out in the first sentence, while in a recount the showing sentences will elaborate on the events of that particular section of the action. It's the micro-equivalent of the old formula for writing an essay: say what you're going to say; say it; say what you just said.

The reason that the showing sentence part of the paragraph is restricted here to two sentences is because more than this is an unrealistic expectation for a beginner writer – they will simply lose the train of thought. Even if the children are really skilled writers, I would advise against letting them write more than three sentences in the main body of the paragraph as we do not want them to go off track with their thought processes (it is better to start a new paragraph with a new idea).

 ## Activity – Paragraphs with Punch (2)

1. Display a telling sentence on the whiteboard that could introduce a paragraph and tell the children that they are going to build a paragraph based on this. For example, a starter might be:

Jack's bedroom was not the tidiest.

The Vikings have a bit of a bad press.

Ashley froze in terror.

It was the ugliest dog I'd ever seen.

It was the most amazing hat in the history of the world.

2. Children work in partnerships to compose the rest of the paragraph. Share some efforts and discuss the effects.

The more fun you can make the paragraph openers, the more room the children will have to play with what follows. What generally happens is that a sense of competition develops with children sparring to come out with the most graphic examples. Encourage this as this sense of enthusiasm will spill over into their writing compositions. More suggestions for paragraph starters appear in Appendix 5.

A Word on Redrafting

Redrafting is the part of the writing process where we look at how we express our ideas and decide whether it is possible to communicate them in a way that is clearer, more interesting or simply different. Very often, however, this is seen as an onerous and time-consuming task where the focus is to restructure every sentence that a child has already written. If we reframe this idea, as with many of the activities suggested above, to show that redrafting can be a quick activity that is not necessarily done for the purpose of fixing something that was wrong with the original work, but simply to convey the information differently, then children will begin to approach their own writing with the same spirit of curiosity and playfulness. Moreover, if we can play with different ways of expressing the ideas contained within just one sentence, then by default, given enough time, the skill can also be applied to a whole composition.

Also, by playing with examples that the children already know have been created by a successful (i.e. published) author, we help promote the idea that even established writer's output can be manipulated to change the effect: we are not trying to 'improve' on their work, simply seeing what might happen if we changed just one small element of it.

All of these messages are important ones as they give children a sense of the possibilities that are open to them as apprentice writers.

Chapter 8: Writing across the Curriculum (Making the most of writing opportunities outside literacy time)

We've given a lot of attention so far to what happens when we focus on developing children's writing muscle during our dedicated literacy time. But we need to remember that the function of writing is to be a tool for recording information and communicating ideas to other people – we write all the time, and for many different purposes, not just when we are consciously practising the skill of writing.

According to OFSTED, '(the problem is) too many pupils, especially older students, do not see English as a subject that affects their daily lives.' The most effective way to embed literacy skills is to present opportunities to practise them in contexts that are meaningful and relevant. This does not mean of course that literacy skills should never be taught in the context of a dedicated lesson (they do need to be in order to give the basic instruction); simply that the skills need to be promoted at any and every opportunity for further practice and application.

It has often been shown that pupils who struggle with the whole writing experience have a view of the subject that confines it to being school-based and academic rather than having almost infinite practical applications in a variety of situations. In this section, we will remind ourselves to guide the children's attention to elements of the writing process, whether the main intended outcome is a report on a science experiment you conducted as a class; a class display about Tudor housing; content for a webpage; or a newsletter to the local community about the new wild environment you are creating at the bottom of the playing field.

Practically all areas of the curriculum require us to record our findings and understanding in some kind of written form. The thing to remember is to consciously make the links between the piece of writing that the children are doing during time dedicated to another curriculum area, and the writing skills you have been practising during literacy time.

 Let's imagine that the children are being asked to collaboratively produce a newspaper that might have been published during the time of the ancient Egyptians. The main assessment focus of this as a piece of topic work will clearly be to notice what the finished product tells us about the children's accumulated understanding of events and concepts associated with ancient Egypt. But while they are engaged in the process, you will be reminding them of what they already know about the features of newspaper reporting: headlines that grab the reader's attention; a first paragraph that gives a basic overview of the story being reported and then other details filled in in chronological order; quotations from eyewitnesses; sensational language choices, and so on.

You may also have been recently working on the children's ability to develop their ideas and to present these in the form of extended sentences. This will then be another opportunity to remind the children to practise this skill. In the same way that when you model and guide writing during literacy time with an absolute clarity of what it is you want the children to be learning (with regard to word level, sentence level, paragraph level skills and whole-text construction), you will be retaining this laser-sharp focus when using writing as a medium for recording ideas and understanding related to other subject areas, or when communicating ideas for a real audience. In the same way that you will have scaffolded your writing tasks to make the learning accessible to everyone and then differentiated to accommodate the children's varying needs in the form of what concrete support needs to be offered so that all the children have the same chance of achieving the desired outcome (planning sheets, writing frames, vocabulary lists, etc.), you will need to provide exactly the same level of support for any task that results in a written end product, no matter what the curriculum focus.

Whatever the content of the children's writing, you will have envisaged the end product as being for a particular purpose (genre), broadly divided into fiction (imaginary recounts or descriptions) or non-fiction (text designed to inform, recount real events, explain, describe, analyse, persuade, argue a case, advise, give an opinion, comment or reflect, or to discuss an issue).

Once the purpose of the intended output is clear, there is some choice about the form that the writing will take (i.e. what it looks like on the page). Possible forms for imaginary writing could include narrative stories, graphic stories, play scripts, letters, fictional diary entries, poems and prose poems. Possible forms for non-fiction writing could include reports, essays, manuals, instructions, letters, fact files, posters, brochures, adverts, articles, blogs or web pages.

All writing genres and forms have conventions and features associated with them that the children will need to be made aware of if they are to be entirely successful at the task. Your job will be to make clear to the children exactly why they are writing (so they can assess whether their work meets its intended purpose), and what features should be evident on the page to help their writing meet that purpose. You will also notice that many pieces of writing have more than one purpose: an information leaflet telling us about the facilities on offer at a new leisure centre could have a sub-text of persuading people to visit; or a report on melting ice caps could include basic facts, an explanation about why it is happening, and a plea for people to do something about it.

The suggestions that follow are meant to be a taster menu of what is possible. The invitation is to have some fun with it. You will be assessing understanding of a much broader range of content than I have space to address here, but once you are confident about what is on offer as regards genres and forms of presenting information, you will have free rein to conjure up an engaging vehicle for writing about anything. The possibilities are limitless and exciting.

History

This assumes we have been studying the Romans – feel free to amend accordingly.

- Would I have preferred to have lived in Roman times or in the modern day? (Balanced argument)

- Advert for Roman baths (Persuasion)

- Speech by Julius Caesar to persuade the British people that they would be better off as part of the Roman Empire (Persuasion)

- Brochure about the opening of the Coliseum (Information with element of persuasion)

- Argument for / against using wild animals in gladiatorial contests (Argument)

- Newspaper article about the eruption of Vesuvius / obliteration of Pompeii (Recount)

- Menu for Roman banquet (Information with element of persuasion)

- Day in the Life of a Roman slave girl / boy (First-person recount)

- Fact sheet about Roman clothing (Information)

- Sales leaflet for a brand-new Roman villa (Information /persuasion)

- Handbook for a newly-conscripted gladiator (Information)

- Collaborative magazine aimed at Roman families (Mixed articles)

- Poster advertising chariot race (Information / persuasion)

- Graphic story based on the eruption of Vesuvius (main character is a child living in Pompeii) (Narrative)

- Fact sheet about Roman technology / innovation (Information)

- Retelling of the story of Romulus and Remus (Narrative)

- Guidebook to Roman gods and goddesses (Information)

Geography

Assuming we have been studying deserts – amend accordingly

- Survival guide to staying alive in the desert (Information / explanation)

- Tourist brochure for Sahara Desert (Information / persuasion)

- Fact sheet about desert animals (Information)

- Day in the life of a Tuareg child (Recount)

- Advert for technologically advanced tent, specially adapted for desert dwelling (Persuasion)

- Adventure story about being lost in the Sahara – present the beginning of the story where you have won a holiday with your parents and somehow, during a rest stop the coach drives off and leaves you behind (Narrative)

- Menu for 'Desert Diner' (Information / persuasion)

- Diary entry by Alexandrine Tinné as she prepares to set off to cross the Sahara (First woman to attempt the expedition in 1869 – unfortunately lost her life before succeeding) (First-person recount)

- Poster presenting facts about main deserts throughout the world (could prepare a duplicated world map annotated to show the locations of main deserts along with text boxes to provide information about them – work collaboratively in partnerships to complete) (Information)

- Comparison of daily life in Sahara and Gobi deserts (Balanced report)

Science

  As a general rule, writing up an experiment will always take the following form: **'What we did…' / 'What happened…' / 'What we learned…'** (Recount).

Assuming a science topic based on 'space' – amend accordingly.

- Newspaper report on first Moon landings (Recount)
- 'Planets' fact file (Information)
- Journey to the Sun (Narrative)
- Diary entry for Yuri Gagarin – about to become first man in space (First-person recount)
- Information leaflet for 'space school' – guidance for prospective space cadets (Information)
- Discursive report about whether or not money should be spent on re-adopting Moon missions (Discussion)
- Poster to show how spacecraft is adapted to accommodate life in space (Information)
- Fact file about Space Station (Information)
- Personal opinion about whether you would / would not like to visit Space Station (Opinion)
- Space poem inspired by photo from Hubble Telescope (Could be performed over theme to '2001') (Poetry)
- Prose poem based on picture of Saturn and its moons (Description)
- Advert for proposed trip to Mars (Information / persuasion)
- Discursive article about likelihood of life on Mars (Balanced argument)
- Argument for / against likelihood of aliens landing on Earth in next ten years (Argument)
- Compare / contrast Jupiter and Mercury (Information / balanced report)
- Report on whether Jupiter would be a suitable place for Earth-dwellers to set up home (Information / opinion)
- Beginning of 'Noah's Ark' story set in 2070 – space craft leaving Earth, destination unknown (Narrative)
- If you could visit any planet, which one would it be? Why? (Opinion)

Art

- Prose poem to describe Rousseau's 'Tiger' or Rene Magritte's 'Day and Night' (Description)

- Letter from Michelangelo to a friend describing his feelings about finishing the ceiling of the Sistine Chapel (First-person recount)

- Opinion piece on radical work of art – e.g. Salvador Dalí's 'The Persistence of Memory' (Opinion)

- Poem based on Van Gogh's 'Starry Night' (Poem)

- First-person recount by Lisa del Giocondo (subject of the Mona Lisa) describing the experience of sitting for Da Vinci – what is the story behind her enigmatic expression? (First-person recount)

- Horror story inspired by Edvard Munch's 'The Scream' (Narrative)

- Prose poem inspired by Van Gogh's 'Café terrace at Night' (Description)

- 'My thoughts at this moment' by the character in Winslow Homer's 'The Gulf Stream' (Monologue)

- Retelling of 'The Fall of Icarus' inspired by Breughel's 'Landscape with the Fall of Icarus' (Recount)

- Mood portrait of Monet's garden based on painting of Japanese bridge and lily pond (Description)

- Reaction piece to Picasso's 'Guernica' (Opinion)

Environment

- Leaflet advocating recycling (Information / persuasion)
- Fact file about diminishing ice caps (Information / argument)
- Speech to challenge people to do their bit to resolve climate change (Argument)
- Advert to campaign to preserve the habitat of polar bears (Persuasion)
- Speech to challenge deforestation of Amazon basin (Argument)
- Discursive report on the pros and cons of drinking bottled water (tap water is contaminated by chemicals vs plastic bottles don't begin to degrade for 100 years) (Balanced argument)
- Report about the plight of the honeybee – why might its numbers be diminishing? / What would be the threat of this? / What can we do to prevent this happening? (Information / explanation)
- If I were the ocean I would feel... (Imaginative description)

RE

- Fact file on world faiths (Information)
- Retelling of important stories from world faiths (Recount)
- Fact file on places of worship (church, mosque, synagogue, temple, etc.) (Information)

PHSE

- Write about a time when your first impression of someone changed after you got to know him or her (Recount / reflection)

- Is honesty always the best policy? (Balanced argument)

- One-week menu for healthy-options school dinners (Information)

- Advice leaflet for children beginning school this September (Information / advice)

- How to be a good friend (Advice)

- Sun-sense poster (Information / advice)

- Healthy eating fact-file (Information / advice)

- Advert to persuade more people to take up sport (Persuasion)

- Discursive report about whether children spent too much time indoors nowadays (Balanced argument)

- Is it better to be young or old? (Opinion)

- Speech encouraging children and old people to spend time together (Persuasion)

- When I am grown-up I will be a _____ then I will be able to _____ (Explanation)

- How I make myself feel better when I'm feeling low (Information / advice)

- My proudest achievement is _____ (Recount / reflection)

- Something I have learned about myself is _____ (Reflection)

- What is the most important quality to you in a friend? Why? (Reflection)

- Stranger danger poster (Information / advice)

- Keep safe during the summer holidays advertising campaign (Information / advice)

- Is watching TV a good or bad thing? (Argument)

- Do you have to spend a lot of money to have fun? (Opinion)

- What do I think the world will be like when I am grown-up? (Description)

- Children shouldn't have to wear school uniforms – discuss (Balanced argument)

- What is your dream for yourself? (Description)

- What is your dream for the world? (Description)

- What are the four most important things in your life? Why? (Description / explanation)

Writing for Real Purposes

It's not possible for every writing task we set to be entirely authentic – i.e. to have a real audience beyond the children's writing buddies and the teacher – as we need a large number of contrived stimuli in order to teach and practise those pre-determined writing skills that we have assessed the children as most urgently needing to acquire next. But there are very good reasons for setting up opportunities for authentic writing wherever they present themselves.

This is an important part of our armoury because writing for a real reason (e.g. a letter to the local council asking that a pedestrian crossing be installed at a dangerous junction, or a book review on Amazon) provides an explicit link between the skill of writing and its real-life application. This is the very thing that OFSTED identified was missing in the experience of many older children. The motivational aspect of writing to a real identified person should also not be underestimated, even if a letter is subsequently ignored.

When writing for a real audience, aspects such as consideration of the tone and the appropriate level of formality most effective in eliciting a desired response is a key factor. If I wrote to my local MP on a matter of pressing concern related to something I had seen reported on the local news, I would not expect the best response if I addressed him in the same way as I might my oldest friend. Being able to adopt a suitably formal tone lends our writing a degree of gravitas and authority: a useful skill indeed if we want to influence others or persuade someone to a course of action by our words. Similarly, if I wrote a contribution for the school newsletter designed to welcome new pupils and their parents to the school and adopted the tone of a crusty old professor, I might well lose my intended audience before they get to the end of what I had wanted to say to them.

Real writers can very occasionally be published authors, but more usually they are simply people who use writing in their daily lives – i.e. most of us – as an effective and efficient means of communication, and as a tool to achieve a desired outcome. These writers compose letters, emails and memos on a daily basis. They may also write personal blogs or websites, song lyrics, online comment in response to something they have read, or online reviews for books and products.

The difference between 'real' writing and writing in response to an artificial prompt isn't necessarily a black and white distinction. Our job as teachers is to help children to see the links. Any activity that has a significance or personal value for the children – and one where they can see exactly why they're doing it – is bound to have a greater impact in terms of motivation and therefore effort applied to the task. It might also have the extra benefit of actually causing something worthwhile to happen in the school or wider environment.

Suggestions for Real Purposes for Writing

- Recount of a trip for school newspaper or class magazine
- Letter of thanks to a visitor
- Letter to a favourite author
- Letter to the council / local paper about an issue of local concern
- Book review / recommendation for classmates
- Contributions to class magazine / newspaper
- Newsletter to parents
- Writing story books to read to younger classes
- Letter to parents about forthcoming trip
- Letter to persuade head teacher to make a change to the school day / school environment / school rules
- Planning research topics for forthcoming trip
- Planning questions to ask a proposed visitor
- Writing film or book review for website (e.g. Amazon)
- Writing product review for manufacturer (either to send to manufacturer or to post online)
- Comments on online news stories
- Content for school website
- Content for class blog
- Content for entrance hall display introducing visitors to the school, its community and its ethos

Chapter 9: How to Mark and Give Feedback

In the not-so-distant past, marking directly translated as a summative assessment: giving a child's piece of work a grade (B+), or at best a grade with some vague generalised statement attached (B+, could do better), and using this to assign a child a position in the class based on a comparison of their effort to their classmates'. Although it might be slightly useful for a child to know how they are performing compared to their peers, it is hardly encouraging (unless the child consistently scores A grades, in which case they almost certainly need more challenging tasks than they are currently being presented with). Even worse, it gives the receiver of the grade no indication of how they might do better on another occasion.

Obviously we do need to mark children's writing. It gives us information about how a child is performing, and we can correct mistakes and misperceptions before they become entrenched. Children also like to know that their work is being read and their ideas valued, parents like it, and of course it provides accountability (telling managers and OFSTED that we are 'on top of things' and generally doing a good job).

But it is not enough simply to draw a smiley face at the bottom (however much we want to encourage children) and leave it at that – if not given specific guidance on what to do next, the work will continue to arrive at exactly the same standard. Neither is it helpful to paste in a list of National Curriculum objectives with ticks next to the indicators that have been demonstrated. The feedback we give to children needs to be simultaneously meaningful, encouraging, constructive and gently challenging.

In order for feedback to work – i.e. improve standards of children's writing – children have to want to improve. This is not as blindingly obvious a statement as it might first appear. You need to ask yourself: what motivates my children to want to get better at writing? Do they feel part of a writing community where they feel encouraged, supported and nurtured to take risks and generally have a go? Do they buy into the apprenticeship approach to writing where we are all (including the teacher) 'learning on the job' by responding to critiquing from peers and teacher, so that they appreciate the value of feedback? Are the children generally encouraged to take ownership of their progress and relate focussed effort to achievement?

Having a real purpose for a piece of writing is also a powerful motivator. Knowing that they are writing a story that will be published in an anthology to be presented to a younger class, or to parents, will instil a sense of pride in the finished work that writing the same story in an exercise book where it will languish until the end of time cannot match.

Feedback is acted on immediately as children reconsider their choices at the point of making them. The teacher can then come back to check that the child has improved on the original version (and make some kind of annotation in the book to show that support had been offered).

The first rule of feedback is that it needs to be immediate (as far as possible) and lead to action. This can be observed at its most effective when children share their work aloud with their partners for general impressions and helpful suggestions for improvement, and when the teacher is circulating whilst children are engaged in writing their first drafts or working on redrafts – he or she is constantly reading over the children's shoulders as they write and stopping them to ask whether they really meant to write what they just did, or gently extending their skills by challenging them to take their writing a step further in terms of complexity of sentence structure or vocabulary choices.

If the feedback is in the form of written marking comments, it is still vital that these are acted upon. Unfortunately, this is the part that is often overlooked in our busy classrooms where the curriculum is oozing out of the cupboards, demanding to be taught in the gap between morning break and lunchtime. But it is only useful if the child is required to do something in response to what they have read.

Ideally, marking needs to be done on the same day that a piece of writing is completed – and certainly no later than the same evening so that the work can be returned on the following morning. I can hear you groaning and asking how you are going to be able to fit this in. But I can assure you that it is a lot easier to do the marking whilst details of the task – and the conversations you had with individual children about it – are still fresh in your mind, as well as making it easier for the children to pick it up again in order to move forward.

When the work is returned the following day (or better still, the afternoon of the same day), children need to be given time – 10 minutes should be enough – to read through what you have written. They can then respond to it by redrafting just one or two sentences after considering your comments about them, and make any mechanical corrections including spelling and punctuation errors that you may have highlighted.

Comments that invite the children to 'try using more adjectives in their writing next time' are ineffectual – by 'next time' the urgency will have disappeared and the children will have difficulty remembering the directive. They need to go back and use more adjectives in a sentence that you have already highlighted for them in this piece of writing – making the invitation very explicit. You will also need to acknowledge with some kind of marking shorthand, when you next take the books in, that you have noticed the new, improved version.

It is not necessary for the child to go back and improve the whole piece of work. This is too daunting a task (unless there is some special reason, such as publication, that merits the amount of time that it would need). The rationale is that, by implication, if a child can improve one sentence in response to a very clear directive about how to do this, then given enough time they would be able to apply this to a longer piece of writing.

All of this will only be as onerous to the children as you present it to be. If you promote the idea that we are all apprentice writers, then by definition, any piece of writing can be seen as a work in progress, and one that is constantly begging to be tweaked and polished as we get it out and hold it up to the light to see where we can enhance its beauty. Once we fully embrace this concept, the only difficult part is deciding when it is 'good enough', and when to stop and allow our project to be shared with the world.

In this paradigm, children will take real pleasure in making their writing efforts as lovingly crafted as possible. You can promote this view of the writing process by coming back to your own writing that you have shared with the children. You can tell them that you have had 'time to sleep on it' and now realise how you could make a sentence better – either by changing or extending its structure or by using alternative vocabulary choices – and redrafting it to reflect this.

The second principle of giving feedback is that it needs to be meaningful, focused and specific. It needs to address questions such as: did this piece of work meet its purpose, and how exactly did it do this? How effective was this piece of work in meeting the purpose, and what did you particularly like about it? How could it be made better (include very precise guidance about exactly how to do this)?

Feedback also needs to show children where they have made spelling or punctuation errors so that these can be corrected. It needs to be written in language that the child can understand and show, by highlighting a particular sentence, where the suggestion for improvement is to be applied. You will need three colours of highlighting pen that you use consistently: one to highlight 'writing triumphs' – where a child has been bold with a vocabulary choice or crafted a complex or particularly effective sentence construction (remember to tell them why it was so impressive); one to highlight sentences which they might have a go at redrafting – along with helpful comments about how to do this; and one to highlight mechanical (spelling and punctuation) errors that need correcting. (Spelling corrections should always be written out in full as this promotes muscle memory for forming the letter patterns correctly on another occasion.)

In general, the comments you provide will include: one that is specifically encouraging ('great use of ellipsis to create a sense of tension'); one that is constructive ('go back and add adjectives to describe the spooky character'); and one that presents an element of challenge and encourages the child to think in greater depth about their writing ('can you describe what the man was doing to make him seem suspicious?'). Bear in mind that this guidance is generic and also needs to be age-appropriate.

All the above relates to giving feedback that will help the children to improve directly as they take ownership of their writing apprenticeship status, but remember that this will equally inform your own planning (Assessment for Learning). If you notice that you are consistently giving feedback that relates for example to using more complex sentences or using cohesive devices within paragraphs to make the sentences flow better, then this should be a focus for your mini-lessons and your shared writing experiences. Formative assessment is as much about guiding the teacher where to take the class next as it is about steering an individual child towards improving their efforts.

Principles of Feedback in a Nutshell

Feedback should:

1. Be immediate and require action

2. Be meaningful (child-friendly) and guide improvement through use of specific invitations for redrafting (improving quality of content)

3. Guide correction of mechanical errors (spelling and punctuation)

Comments should:

1. Encourage (and say why something is good)

2. Be constructive (say how to make a sentence better)

3. Challenge (extend the child to think about their writing in greater depth)

 Feedback needs to be pertinent to this piece of writing (not referring to a set of generic objectives) and relate to sentences (or vocabulary choices) that you have highlighted.

Use three colours of highlighting:

1. A 'Writing Triumph'

2. An invitation to redraft

3. Spelling and punctuation errors

Chapter 10:
A Note about Boys

You may already intuitively feel that, for whatever reason, boys tend to struggle more than girls to do well at writing. This has been confirmed by research, and the gap between boys' and girls' attainment is wider than it is for reading.

Why is this? We are giving the same amount of attention to both boys and girls within our classrooms and they are responding to the same input.

It would be a sweeping generalisation to suggest that all girls are motivated by wanting to please their teachers, and because they value writing as an activity that we do for its own sake. But there is an element of truth in this statement, meaning that many girls are intrinsically wired to do better in our traditional classroom settings. For boys, we need to give more careful thought about how to make writing assignments both meaningful and accessible to them, so that they see the task as relevant and give value to the quality of their finished product.

According to HMI ('Yes he Can – Schools where Boys Write Well' 2003 and backed up by further evidence in 2005), the factors identified as making a difference to boys in the learning environment can be broken down into the following categories:

1. quality of teaching (teacher expertise and modelling of grammar skills in the context of writing tasks)

2. school-level factors (whether or not writing is promoted as an exciting and high-status activity)

3. classroom environment (whether ICT and media resources are used effectively to introduce visually exciting writing tasks)

4. classroom management (behavioural management and general environment)

5. factors relating to the ways lessons are actually delivered (e.g. whether children are allowed to pick their own story topic or whether they all have to write about the same thing)

The suggestions that follow are all based on research about task presentation and classroom management, and also echo guidance by OFSTED and ESTYN based on observations of schools where boys did particularly well at writing. Many of the points will appeal equally to girls, so we need not worry about alienating them in the process of making our teaching more accessible to boys. And many are probably what we already know to be characteristic of good teaching. But it is always useful to review our current practice on an on-going basis and check whether we are offering our children the full range of strategies that we know will impact on their learning and therefore on the quality of their finished writing.

Expert Teaching

The first factor that will influence boys' performance is an obvious one: quality of teaching. How reliable and meticulous is the instruction that they receive? Be reassured that if you follow the guidance given in the rest of this book, the strategies that follow will all have been taken care of.

First and foremost, teachers need to be highly knowledgeable and enthusiastic about the subject of writing. If this is not your natural forte then steps can be taken to make it so. Read up on the technicalities of grammar and sentence construction, and if it is not your natural passion to write, wear your actor's hat, in the same way as you would to share other knowledge and skills with the children. The best role model the children can have is a teacher who shares their writing attempts with them and whom they sometimes witness writing alongside them in the same way as they might witness you enjoying reading alongside them.

Next, you need to be smart about what impact exactly you want your shared writing time to have on the children's writing. Do you want them to concentrate on making sure the verbs in their sentences always correspond to the subjects they relate to? Or maybe the children are proficient at constructing complex sentences linked by conjunctions such as 'because', but you would like them to start using a wider range of subordinating conjunctions? Or do you want to show how a writer uses variations of standard and non-standard English in characters' dialogue?

Whatever it is that you would like to see as the next step in the children's writing is exactly the skill that you need to focus on, in microscopic detail, during your shared writing time. You will then need to remind the children that this is also the focus for their first drafts and when they come to redrafting (or editing if it is a punctuation or other mechanical issue). Reward them when you see them doing this.

Boys in particular are unlikely to pick up grammar rules, the subtleties of language features and vocabulary choices, or the varied menu of clause and sentence construction options available to them simply by a process of osmosis from reading. You need to teach all of these in words of one syllable, to notice them and draw attention to them when you come across them in shared reading time, and to make full use of shared writing opportunities and mini-lessons within longer writing periods. As we have already discussed, grammar taught outside the context of writing is a necessary preparation for passing a grammar test, but it will not impact on the quality of children's writing unless its teaching is an integral part of the writing process.

Boys respond well when lessons are pacey, with a brisk beginning, followed by a varied selection of activities that are delivered at an appropriate speed for them not to lose interest, and interspersed with frequent reviews of what they have just done. They also perform well when activities are highly scaffolded, i.e. broken down into bite-sized chunks, with a good balance between supported and independent activities.

And it goes without saying that all teaching needs to be based on frequent assessment of children's individual progress and meticulous tweaking of next teaching steps based on your findings.

Classroom Management

All children will respond well to the following strategies, but meticulous attention to making sure that these are well-managed will go a long way to making sure that the boys in your classroom make progress that matches the girls'.

Adopt a policy of prompt marking of children's writing (overnight at the latest) with detailed and concrete feedback both about what has been done well and the next steps for improvement. This needs to be accompanied with the expectation that feedback requires action, whether this is to redraft a sentence that you have highlighted with a suggestion about how to do this, to choose a more interesting synonym for a word that you have highlighted, or maybe to expand a highlighted noun with more information about it.

Boys need to know that they are responsible for the standard of their own work: they need to be involved in an ongoing individual review process based on your assessments and observations of their strengths and weaknesses, and to be actively involved in collaborative target setting and monitoring of progress. Boys in particular will want to be reminded of the correlation between making an effort in the areas that you highlight for them, and results in the form of improved standards.

You will have your own school policy relating to behaviour management. But it is worth noting that boys do better when a deliberately non-confrontational method is chosen: ignoring bad behaviour as far as it is safe to do so; praising and rewarding positive behaviour whenever it is observed; and making very clear the reasons why behaviour rules might be in place and why certain actions – or inactions – are not acceptable (i.e. what is the impact of them).

Boys also like predictability. They like to know that the expectation of how things are done stays the same from day to day, and exactly what the rewards and consequences are of different actions.

Making Writing a School-wide Focus

Giving school-wide recognition to the importance of writing – both for teachers and for children – has been shown to have a huge impact in raising standards for all children, but especially for boys. Being part of a whole school where children are encouraged to read for pleasure (in all genres) and where all children are expected to write frequently and at length (including as homework assignments) results in children who are exposed to a wide variety of writing models and who develop writing stamina.

Teachers need to place importance not just on skills acquisition, but on promoting pleasure and enjoyment in writing. You can do this perhaps by allocating periods where you write alongside the children, or by allowing a certain amount of free-rein as to the format of writing assignments (particularly for homework). Perhaps the children might like to create an animated story book or a magazine or an information poster that they can work on at home over a period of time and then bring in and share with the rest of the class (or this activity can be completed during 'golden-time' where the children earn chunks of time which they can use for free-choice activities).

Boys like it when writing is a high-status activity: maybe a regular school-wide writing challenge issued during assembly, or a competition where the winners get chosen to be published in a school magazine or anthology. Picking aspirational role models in terms of visiting successful children's authors, or other motivational figures who can talk to the children about the importance of being good writers to their current status, is also motivating for boys who might otherwise struggle to see the value attached to improving their skills.

Implementing a programme of mentoring by older boys for boys who are struggling with writing has also been shown to be effective at improving standards. Boys need to be reminded that writing is not necessarily a 'fluffy' activity and that it has real and relevant applications that are directly meaningful to them.

Creating a 'Boy-friendly' Classroom Environment

What things can we do on a day-to-day basis to promote boys' progress in writing, and what resources can we use to support this?

Two main strategies we can put in place throughout the day, not just during designated 'literacy' time, are using talk to support writing (thinking aloud), and using writing to support thought (note-taking and planning tools).

As part of the scaffolding or breaking-down of writing tasks, one important factor in the modelling process is articulating how writers think. Because we are good writers, we tend to operate, as we do for reading, at a level of 'unconscious competency'.

In order to teach children to think like writers we need to make them aware how good writers think. It is not enough to make decisions associated with writing in the privacy of our own heads; we need the thoughts to be articulated out loud so that the children can hear them. For example, if I am modelling writing a story for my class, I might have a conversation with myself regarding what I shall write about. I will show the children how I come up with ideas, select one as being more viable than the others, and then go on to develop it so that my story gains flesh. In the same way, I will encourage the children to talk to their partners about their own stories, testing out their ideas on each other before committing themselves to developing it on the page (rehearsal for writing). Similarly, I will demonstrate to the children how I use writing to record my thinking processes: how to take notes using key words only and omitting superfluous detail and using the same technique to plan writing (using the minimum number of words necessary to allow me to remember what it is I shall write about). This will provide them with a useful tool for efficiently recording ideas.

Allow plenty of time at the pre-writing stage of the process for children to explore and develop their ideas before instructing them to begin writing. This way, the less confident writers won't be overwhelmed by lack of structure to their ideas, and the already confident will be sufficiently 'warmed-up' to develop their ideas with a level of detail that wouldn't have been accessible to them before.

As an aside on the above train of thought, remember that boys are often suspicious of 'flowery language' and don't find the idea attractive of using five words where one would do the job. Remember that there are many writing genres where conciseness and clarity are desirable qualities, and give praise when these are demonstrated in an appropriate context.

Boys like to know that they are doing their writing for a real purpose, so build in plenty of opportunities for presentation and performance (i.e. they know they will have a real audience). This might be intimidating to begin with if this is not something they are used to, but eventually they will grow in confidence and rise to the challenge, improving the quality of their written preparation along the way, and – as a by-product – developing their oracy skills and self-esteem. Write letters to real people wherever the opportunity arises, or write for publication in class newspapers, newsletters or anthologies. Anything, so long as they are writing!

Use all the ICT facilities available in your classroom: visual media on the whiteboard for introducing or building up to the activity; interactive whiteboards for teaching mini-lessons within the activity or for altering text (when modelling redrafting or editing); or children's laptops for publishing the finished work. All these will make the task more appealing to the technologically impressionable boys.

Delivering Lessons that Boys will Love

As we have said, boys respond to highly structured, well-focussed lessons with clearly-stated objectives (expressed in language that the children understand), delivered at a well-maintained pace, with clear stages to the learning, and with variation in the activities with plenty of time to reflect and review between stages. Many of these stages will include paired or collaborative tasks that lead up to the production of more independent work, including tasks where children talk out their ideas with each other.

Boys need to have a clear explanation of the features of good writing in whatever genre they are being asked to replicate – think of it as having a recipe book with clear instructions to follow. They also write better when given planning forms, writing frames, story maps or other visual organisers to help them structure their thinking, or sentence stems to get them started. These can be given to the whole class or modified to make them more appropriate for groups of children or individual children within the group.

Give the children prompts based on TV programmes that they enjoy, a film that will be familiar to them, or computer games, web pages, email or blogs. It doesn't matter how you capture their imagination for writing; it just matters that they are enthused. Allow the children sometimes to choose their own topics for story writing – boys often have a fascination for certain genres such as horror, sporting stories or adventure that the girls won't necessarily share. The format of the writing is not the factor that will define it: the judgement will be made about the quality of the writing within.

Use drama activities wherever possible to role-play or enact scenes from a text that you are reading together, to explore character thoughts and feelings, to explore the cause and effect nature of narrative and to develop narrative in preparation for writing. Use techniques such as hot-seating, freeze-framing and thought-tapping to 'get inside the skin' of a narrative so that children feel they have real ownership of it before they begin to write about it.

Also, boys seem to like writing poetry. This might seem at odds with their interest in technological and fact-driven media. But if you think about writing poetry, there is a lot of permission attached to the form, including a greater sense of freedom with sentence and clause construction. This allows children to try out structures in a non-threatening way because poetic structures cannot be 'wrong' – they only sound more or less pleasing depending on the words chosen and the order in which they are put together. Give the children plenty of opportunity to read poems aloud: this way they get a feel for the flow of language and the potential for language-play.

Use emotionally powerful texts or visual media to prompt writing. You will need a good 'hook' to get the boys into the writing water. But once they are there they will swim, as long as you provide them with clear instructions for what to do at each stage and equip them with the 'lifejackets' they need to support the process (tools such as planning forms, vocabulary banks or writing frames).

Allow plenty of time to reflect on their work at each stage and improve on it. Impress upon the children that all writing is a work in progress. No one expects perfection at any stage in the process – a polished effort is something of value and in which they should take pride.

Whenever possible, set up opportunities for the children to share their finished writing with a real audience: an author's chair at the front of the class for reading aloud to the whole class; going into other classrooms to share story time; or contributing to a class newspaper, story book, display board, blog, or anything that is going to be read by someone other than you. Look for writing competitions that the children can enter and opportunities to contribute letters to magazines, local papers and TV shows. Encourage them to write for fun and in their spare time; or to create mad and complicated plotlines for a class soap opera. Or to write letters: to you, to each other, to a famous person – to anyone at all!

If their creative content is sometimes predictable or uninspired, don't worry – that will come. Concentrate instead on building a solid repertoire of word, sentence and paragraph skills that can be applied to any writing situation later on, and praise the children to the sky when a new skill is mastered.

In this way, you are sculpting real writers: writers who are independently motivated, equipped with the skills necessary to communicate their ideas, and with a variety of appropriate and entertaining writers' voices which they can adapt to any purpose and audience. And better still, what if we could sculpt these same children into adolescents who can respond to the question: 'Am I a good writer?' with a definite 'Yes!', and to the question: 'Do I like writing?' with an 'Of course I do!' or 'Doesn't everybody?'.

Don't Forget to Celebrate Success!

Whatever the children produce in response to your encouragement, the essential thing is to make a celebration out of their creative endeavours. Yes, there will always be improvements to make – that is the nature of learning a craft – but never allow the 'could be better if's to overwhelm the 'what a great writer you're becoming's.

The point of the experience we are creating for the children is that they are apprentice writers. They must be given a space in which to experiment, to take risks with their developing craft, and get it wrong before they begin (more often than not) to get it right.

Recognise when a child has taken a risk with their new skills and compliment them on this (even if, at the same time, suggesting how something could be 'tweaked' to even greater effect).

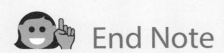 # End Note

None of what we have covered will result in progress overnight. But with persistence and a positive attitude, it is possible to have your whole class actively engaged in writing lessons within a very short period of time, with the payoff in terms of accelerated writing progress following shortly thereafter. And then, once the children begin to see the impact in terms of progress, they will be even more motivated to continue to improve their skills.

The other thing that has been shown overwhelmingly to make a difference in terms of writing impact is to keep the focus of writing progress very much as a whole-school priority. The more that writing activities and achievements can be 'bigged-up' and celebrated at a whole-school level, the more the children will be motivated to improve. But don't worry too much if this is not a possibility within your own school environment; having you as a writing cheerleader and coach will make a huge difference to the children's chances of success.

Appendix one - List of Co-ordinating Conjunctions

and

or

but

for

so

yet

nor

Co-ordinating conjunctions join clauses of equal weight (independent clauses) in a compound sentence (I like apples but I do not like bananas).

(N.B.: The word 'then' is often used in the context of being a co-ordinating conjunction – followed by a comma, unlike the examples above – although, to be pedantic, it is actually a conjunctive adverb.)

Appendix two - List of Subordinating Conjunctions

after

although

as

as if

because

before

even if

if

once

since

so

that

though

unless

until

when

even though

Subordinating conjunctions join clauses where the clause containing the conjunction is dependent on the other clause in order to make sense of it (I like Milly <u>even though she is quite opinionated</u>).

(N.B.: this list is not completely exhaustive but these are the most common examples.)

Appendix three - List of Conjunctive Adverbs to Structure Argument

also

anyway

besides

consequently

finally

first

for example

for instance

furthermore

however

indeed

in fact

instead

in the same way

meanwhile

moreover

now

of course

next

secondly

on the other hand

otherwise

similarly

so far

to sum up

until then

still

then

therefore

Conjunctive adverbs are used to linked ideas together – either to link a sentence to the one preceding it or to transition to another paragraph. (Many of the adverbs listed on the following page can also be used for the same purpose in different text types.)

Appendix four - List of Adverbs

Adverbs of time – tell us when the action takes place:

today	next week	yesterday	earlier	last year
after that	later	previously	soon	once

Adverbs of place – tell us where the action happens:

here	there	everywhere	nowhere	all around
downstairs	above	nearby	far away	inside

Adverbs of direction – tell us which way the action is travelling:

up	down	north	sideways	homewards

Adverbs of manner – tell us how the action happens (they commonly, but do not always, end in –ly):

fast	slowly	well	loudly	hard	carefully

Adverbs of frequency – tell us how often the action happens:

often	never	sometimes	always	seldom	usually

Adverbs of intensity or degree – tell us the extent of what we are describing:

very	quite	completely	absolutely	a little	nearly

Adverbs of possibility / probability – tell us the likelihood of something occurring:

certainly	definitely	maybe	perhaps	possibly	obviously

Appendix five - Examples of Telling Sentences to Introduce Paragraphs with Punch

- The princess was not exactly beautiful.

- Cedric wasn't your usual idea of a dragon-slayer.

- The Vikings were not known for fastidious personal hygiene.

- The cat was fatter than any other I'd ever seen.

- The room was most-definitely haunted.

- The film was ridiculously funny.

- The woman looked very suspicious.

- The dog was vicious – I knew that at once.

- The cake was the most delicious I've ever tasted.

- His shoes were extraordinary.

- His voice was unbearable.

- That summer was the best I've ever known.

- I'm not feeling so good this morning.

- I knew it was going to be a bad day.

- Auntie Zelda is quite an unusual person.

- The car was really fast.

- The journey seemed to last forever.

- The painting wouldn't be to everyone's taste.

- The fox was a beautiful creature.

- The fabric is exquisite.

- The ring looked expensive.

- The banquet was sumptuous beyond belief.

- The book was gripping.

- Her laugh had to be heard to be believed.

- The teddy bear looked as if it had been well-loved.

- The house looked uncared-for.

- The water looked dangerous.

- The crocodile looked mean.

- He was mad about Manchester United.

- Eleanor clearly wasn't interested in what Marco had to say.

- The ice cream is very cold.

- The sunset is beautiful.

- Deirdre wasn't feeling very confident about appearing on the X-Factor.

- The baby seemed to like Jack.

- Arthur didn't think he'd done his best in the test.

- Sam hated his new jumper.

- Jess was insanely jealous.

- The aeroplane hardly looked as if it would be able to get off the ground.

- The yoghurt didn't look too fresh.

- Katie wasn't widely liked.

- The dog looks so happy it might burst.

- I've eaten too much dinner.

- The new teacher looked terrifying.

- Granny's cooking is awful.

- The bag was heavy beyond belief.

- Shanaz's suitcase was packed to bursting point.

- The table was groaning with delicacies.

- The creature is very strange.

- Taylor had to be the cleverest child on the planet.

- I love that story.

- Kittens are the cutest animals around.

- Timothy had a rather strange hairdo.

- I don't think that machine looks very safe.

- Simon's feet were huge.

- Ali hates spiders.

- It's so hot today.

- Not even her parents could have described Shiv as lovely.

- Lauren likes shoes very much.

- Jon's taste in clothes is not exactly ordinary.

- The medicine was the worst thing I'd ever tasted.

- The swimming pool didn't look very inviting.

- The monster was fearsome.

- Tamina was putting on a good show of not being well enough for school.

- The secret was on the tip of my tongue to tell Adele.

- Freddie was mean.

- The suspense was killing me.

- Mrs Henley's new perfume was somewhat overpowering.

- He felt he would die of thirst.

- The parrot was extremely rude.

- No expense had been spared in the building of the palace.

- I am so tired.

- I'd love to have a holiday in the Caribbean.

- It was a cosy little cottage.

- Sometimes, I think Mum can read my mind.

- I knew I just had to have the bicycle.

- The video game was very realistic.

- Francis didn't look all that strong to me.

- He was a brilliant footballer.

Recipes for Writing Genres

Instructions

Structure of writing:

1. Give a title that makes clear what you are doing / making

   - **How to make Jam Tarts**

2. List all materials / ingredients needed

   Be specific:

   - **plain flour**

   Give quantities:

   - **200g sultanas**

3. List all the stages of what needs to be done
   Number the stages /(or) use time connectives

   - **next, after that, finally**

4. Suggest what you could do with the finished product

   - **Leave to cool and enjoy**

 ### Style tips:

- Use second person (you will need)
- Use imperative verbs (stir for five minutes, cut into four pieces)
- Write clearly and in as few words as possible (no 'flowery' language choices!)
- Use technical words and phrases
- Be precise
- Use simple sentences

Information (Non-chronological Report)

Structure of writing:

1. Give a general introduction about the thing you are writing about
Describe your subject

- **Polar bears are large carnivorous mammals that live in the Arctic.**

2. Paragraphs give information about a different aspect of your subject

- **Habitat, food, family groups, hibernation**

Use sub-headings if desired to introduce topic of new paragraph
Develop the ideas – give details to interest the reader

3. Write a conclusion

- **Summarise the known facts**

- **Address the reader directly if appropriate**

 ## Style tips:

- Use third person (it, he, she, they)
- Use present tense
- Use technical words and phrases related to subject
- Stick to facts
- Use formal language
- Include active and passive sentence structures

First-person Recount (e.g. Diary)

Structure of writing:

1. Set the scene (what happened, who, where, when, etc.)

2. Describe the events in the order in which they happened – include details of thoughts and feelings about each event

- **Events leading up to the main event (why it happened)**
- **Events following main event (consequences)**

Use time connectives to give a sense of when things happened in relation to each other

- **Soon after**
- **In the afternoon**
- **As it started to get dark**
- **Later that day**

3. Finish with some kind of reflective comment

 What did you learn from the experience?

 Style tips:

- Use first person (I)
- Use past tense
- Use emotive vocabulary to let the reader know how you were feeling at each point (e.g. powerful verbs – I yelled, I slunk, I whooped; nouns that imply a judgement – traitor, supermum, snitch)
- Include plenty of details to flesh out the story

Newspaper Report

Structure of writing:

1. Set the scene (what happened, who, where, when etc.)

2. Describe the events in the order in which they happened

- **Events leading up to the main event (why it happened)**
- **Events following main event (consequences)**

Use time connectives to give a sense of when things happened in relation to each other

- **Yesterday**
- **At 3.00pm**
- **Two hours later**

Include quotes from eyewitnesses

- **Say who is giving the quote (Mrs Peters, school secretary, aged 35)**
- **Put speech marks round the words quoted**
- **Quotes should say how the witness felt about what they saw**

3. Finish with some kind of reflective comment

▶ **What can we learn from the experience?**

 ## Style tips:

- Use third person (he, she, they)
- Use past tense
- Use 'sensational' or exaggerated language choices (e.g. emotive noun phrases – terrified tot, plucky pensioner, shivering puppy)
- Include plenty of details to flesh out the story and give interest
- Compose a 'cheesy' headline that sums up the main event

Explanation

Structure of writing:

1. Introduction that outlines the current situation / introduces the process to be explained

- **Many scientists are concerned that global warming is reaching crisis point**
- **You may wonder how a beautiful butterfly is able to emerge from something as unlikely as a caterpillar?**

2. Break the information into clear steps that explain how the process works

List the causes and describe the effects at each stage

- **because of this**
- **as a result**
- **so**
- **because**
- **therefore**

3. Write a conclusion

- **Summarise the facts**
- **Address the reader directly if appropriate**
- **Make a prediction about what might happen if nothing is done to resolve situation if this is appropriate**

 ## Style tips:

- Use third person (it, he, she, they)
- Use action words
- Use present tense
- Use technical words and phrases related to subject
- Stick to facts
- Use formal / authoritative language
- Include active and passive sentence structures
- Include relevant details

Argument

Structure of writing:

1. Introduction that outlines your argument

- **What is my proposal?**
- **Why is it so important?**

2. Paragraphs develop a single point that supports the main argument

- **Present supporting evidence**
- **Give examples**
- **Include statistics**
- **Suggest that public opinion is on your side (many people think, most people would agree)**

Use causal connectives

- **as a result**
- **because of this**
- **subsequently**

Use addition of ideas connectives

- **secondly**
- **furthermore**
- **lastly**

3. Write a conclusion

- **Restate why your argument is so important**
- **Make a prediction about what might happen if your argument is rejected**
- **Appeal directly to the reader**

 ## Style tips:

- Use third person (it, he, she, they)
- Use present tense
- Use modal verbs (will, should, could, ought)
- Stick to facts
- Keep the argument logical and easy to follow
- Use formal / authoritative language

- Include active and passive sentence structures
- Use emotive vocabulary that supports your cause
- Include rhetorical questions
- Make generalised statements (not personal)

Balanced Argument (Discussion)

Structure of writing:

1. Introduction that outlines the discussion topic

- **What are the opposing points of view?**
- **Why are both points of view worthy of consideration?**

2. Paragraphs develop considerations related to the topic giving equal weight to arguments both for and against

- **Present supporting evidence**
- **Give examples**
- **Include statistics**

! Remember to keep the coverage balanced – if you present an argument for something, you must, at least, give recognition to the fact that not everyone will agree with this.

Use addition of ideas connectives

- **similarly, furthermore, in the same way**

Use connectives that introduce a counter-view

- **however, on the other hand, in contrast**

3. Write a conclusion

- **Restate the main arguments both for and against the issue**
- **Invite the reader to make up their own mind on the issue**

 ## Style tips:

- Use third person (it, he, she, they)
- Use present tense
- Use future tense and modal verbs (would, should, could, ought)
- Use technical words and phrases related to subject
- Stick to facts

- Keep the argument logical and easy to follow
- Use formal / authoritative language
- Include active and passive sentence structures
- Make generalised statements (not personal)

Story

Structure of writing:

1. Set the scene
- Begin with dialogue, action or description

2. Describe the main story events
- Give plenty of details to interest the reader
- Mix action and dialogue
- Make it clear that actions have consequences (something causes something else to happen)
- Lead up to a main problem that needs to be resolved

3. Use time connectives
- one morning
- later that evening
- two minutes later
- as the children were walking home
- at the stroke of midnight

4. Finish by
- Showing how the main problem is resolved
- Showing that the main problem has got worse
- Leaving the reader in suspense (you keep them guessing about what happened in the end)

 Style tips:

- Usually third person (he, she, they)
- Past or present tense used consistently
- Use 'wow' words
- Use mixture of long and short sentences
- Include details about the things you describe
- Use a variety of sentence openers
- Use adverbs to give extra information about characters' thoughts and feelings
- Use standard English unless writing dialogue
- Use pronouns and varied references to the same thing (Sam, he, the boy, the youngster)

Features of an Adventure Story

(As for story writing plus):

Set your story in a real place

Use lifelike characters

- Somewhere familiar where an unexpected catastrophe occurs

- Somewhere where there is danger from the environment

- Real people who behave heroically in the face of danger

- Villains who try to make the situation worse for their own ends

 **Adventure story tips:**

- Story events could conceivably happen (even if not very likely)

- Hint at adverse events to come

- Use short sentences to keep the pace moving / build up excitement

- Use cliffhangers to keep the reader hooked into the action

- Main problem gets worse and worse before it is finally resolved

Features of Traditional Tale / Fairy Story

1. Begin with a reference to the fact that the story happened a very long time ago

- Once upon a time
- One day, long ago
- One day, in the far-off mists of time

2. Set your story in a vague, faraway land

- In a kingdom, many miles from here
- In a castle
- In a forest

3. Use stock characters, rich and poor, good and evil

- King, queen, prince, princess, rich merchant
- Woodcutter, huntsman, servant
- Witch, wicked step-mother, wolf, troll, goblin, dragon, giant

4. Story includes magic – things that cannot be true

- Wishes are granted
- Curses, wicked spells put in place

5. Character goes on a quest that involves a journey and many dangers and challenges

- To find something
- To win something
- To prove something

6. Things happen in threes
Characters are set tests that show whether they are worthy to go any further

- Nothing is as it seems
- There may be a question to answer or a riddle to solve

7. A difficult problem is resolved by the end of the story – promise of happiness for the main characters

- They all lived happily ever after

Features of a Spooky Story

Set your story in a real place that people might have reservations about visiting

- Graveyard, attic, dungeon, cellar, old castle, derelict house

Set your story at night-time / twilight

- Dark, foggy, midnight, full moon, bad weather, shadows, no electricity, no lights

Use a mixture of lifelike characters and 'spooky' characters

- Zombies
- Ghosts,
- Vampires,
- Werewolves, monsters

Start by describing events that could conceivably happen and 'spooky' characters

- Get locked in attic by mistake, visit graveyard for a dare, get lost in dungeon during trip to castle

Give hints that things are not as they seem

- Strange noises, things disappearing or moving, feeling of dread, main character finds himself alone

 Spooky story tips:

- Create fear – what is unknown is scarier than what is known
- Build up suspense, use element of surprise to shock reader
- Use description to support the creepy setting (creaky stairs, trailing cobwebs, trembling legs)
- Leave the reader guessing how the story ends (may well be a bad ending)
- Main problem gets worse and worse before it is finally resolved

Progression of Writing Skills

Use the following list to decide which skills to focus on for your writing sessions. You can choose more than one focus at a time – e.g. a word level skill, a punctuation skill and a sentence / paragraph skill – but make one a primary focus that you model extensively during shared writing time according to the children's current and most pressing needs. Make the other(s) secondary areas that you also remind the children to check for in addition to the primary focus as they are writing independently.

Be aware that the children will almost certainly not progress at the same rate for every type of skill, so focus on the next level of learning for each discrete strand rather than trying to keep the progress completely level across the board. And keep in mind that, for example, some punctuation skills will lend themselves directly to certain sentence constructions, and that different spelling rules will be associated with, for example, different tense formation, so there will also be explicit links between some of the strands.

I have included guidance about the year group expectations associated with the National Curriculum, not for it to be followed slavishly as it is more important to respond to the children's learning needs from where they actually are, but to flag up a warning if children are falling significantly behind in one area (in which case, this will need immediate attention to remedy).

Year One

Word Level	Sentence Level	Paragraph Level	Punctuation
Simple vocabulary choices (man, dog)	Simple sentence construction (I like my hair.)		Separation of words with spaces
Verb suffix '-ed'	Introduction to simple past tense		Full stops to end sentences
Plural noun suffixes (dogs, cats, wishes)	Subject / verb agreement within sentence	Sequencing sentences to form short narrative	Capital letters to begin sentences
Pronouns 'he', 'she', 'it' etc. to avoid repetition of nouns	Use of 'and' to join clauses within sentence	Longer narrative constructions	Capital letter for 'I'
Proper nouns (names, days of week etc.)	Use of 'then' to join clauses within a sentence		Capital letters for proper nouns
Use of adjectives to describe a noun	Use of 'so' to join clauses within a sentence	Time connectives 'then' and 'next' to begin a sentence	Introduction to question marks
More interesting vocabulary choices ('amazing' rather than 'nice')			Introduction to exclamation marks
Verb suffix '-ing'	Introduction to continuous present or past tense		
Introduction to irregular plural nouns (men, children)			
Negative verb or adjective prefix 'un-'			

Year Two

Word Level	Sentence Level	Paragraph Level	Punctuation
Determiners 'a' / 'an' and 'the'	Consistently accurate sentence constructions (subject / verb agreement; correct choice of 'a' or 'an')	Correct and consistent choice of present or past tense within text	Consistent use of capital letters, full stops, question marks and exclamation marks to demarcate sentences
Simple prepositions of place or time ('to', 'on', 'under', 'in', 'after' etc.)	Simple prepositional phrases ('I looked under the bed.')	Continuous forms of past or present tense used to make clear when actions happened	
Comparative adjectives ('-er') and superlative adjectives ('-est')	Longer noun phrases (two adjectives plus noun)	More time connectives 'first', 'later', 'after that'	Commas to separate items in a list
Irregular comparative and superlative adjectives ('good', 'better', 'best'; 'bad', 'worse', 'worst')	Prepositional phrases to give extra information about a noun ('the man in the moon')	Time-specific time connectives ('next day', 'in the evening', 'two hours later')	Apostrophes for contraction ('can't', 'don't')
Non-generic noun choices ('Ferrari', 'Alsatian')	Subordination using 'because'	Writing longer narratives with phrases that signal beginning ('One day…') or ending (e.g. 'In the end…')	Apostrophe for contraction – 'it's'
Adverbs of manner ('-ly')	Use of 'but' to join clauses within a sentence	Adding extra details to extend an idea or story point	Apostrophes for singular possession ('the girl's purse')
More interesting verb choices ('yelled' instead of 'said')	Subordination using 'if'		'it's' / 'its'
Formation of adjectives using '-ful' ('careful')	Beginning to play with word order in a sentence for interest and effect		Introduction to inverted commas for speech
Formation of nouns using suffixes '-ness' or '-er' ('kindness', 'helper')	Beginning to use a variety of sentence types: statements, questions and commands within narrative		
Compound nouns ('chimneypot', 'whiteboard')	Subordination using 'that'		
Specific determiners 'this', 'that'	Imperative verb forms ('give me that pen')		

Year Three

Word Level	Sentence Level	Paragraph Level	Punctuation
Using a range of prefixes to make nouns and adjectives ('supermarket', 'antidote', 'automatic')	Present perfect tense ('she has gone out')	Ideas extended with extra sentences that follow on from topic sentence	Inverted commas to punctuate speech
Use of technical language where appropriate ('chainsaw', 'booster rocket', 'breed of dog')	Past perfect tense ('She had gone out')	Ideas developed and grouped into sections	Effective punctuation of lists including no final comma before the 'and'
Selecting words from a common word family for effect ('solve', 'solution', 'dissolve')	Clauses linked by conjunctions that express time, place or cause ('when', 'before', 'after', 'while')	Heading and sub-headings to aid presentation of ideas	
Adverbs to express time, place or cause ('soon', 'here', 'therefore')	Use of a time adverb ('earlier', 'later', 'recently')	Adverbs for addition of ideas ('also', 'furthermore', 'as well as')	
More prepositions of place ('above', 'behind', 'opposite', 'on the other side')	Use of an adverb of frequency ('once', 'always', 'sometimes')	Adverbs of contrast ('but', 'in contrast', 'however', 'on the other hand')	
Prepositions to express time or cause ('during', 'because of')	Use of an adverb of manner ('sadly', 'cheerfully')		
Quantifying words ('any', 'enough', 'less', 'more', 'a few')	Consistent subject / verb agreement for the verbs 'to be', 'to do' and 'to have' (including the negative)		
Use of language for effect	Complex sentences joined with conjunctions 'although', 'even if', 'until'		

Year Four

Word Level	Sentence Level	Paragraph Level	Punctuation
Connectives for exemplification ('for instance', 'such as')	Fragmented sentences for effect (for realistic dialogue)	Paragraphs based on topic sentence to organise ideas	Inverted commas plus other punctuation to demarcate direct speech
Connectives for concluding ('to sum up', 'in conclusion')	Switching between standard and non-standard English as appropriate (for dialogue)	Use of repetition for effect	Apostrophes for plural possession
Use of powerful verbs that give a sense of how a character is feeling	Adverbial phrases of time, place or manner to start sentences	Appropriate choice of noun or pronoun to aid cohesion and avoid repetition	Commas after fronted adverbials
Possessive pronouns ('yours', 'mine', 'ours', 'hers', 'his')	Beginning a sentence with a verb ending '-ing'	Using range of conjunctions and connectives to avoid repetition	
More prepositions of place ('above', 'behind', 'opposite', 'on the other side')	Changing the order of phrases or clauses within a sentence for effect		
Similes	Starting a sentence with a simile		
Adverbs to modify adjectives and other adverbs	Modal verbs 'could', 'would', 'should'		
Specific determiners 'these', 'those'	Sentences extended with noun phrases including both adjectives and prepositional phrases ('the horrible bully with the red face')		
Adjectives created from past participles of verbs ('exhausted', 'excited')	Continuous past perfect tense ('he had been running')		

Year Five

Word Level	Sentence Level	Paragraph Level	Punctuation
Converting nouns or adjectives into verbs using suffixes ('-ate', '-ise', '-ify')	Starting a sentence with a subordinate clause	Using devices to build cohesion within a paragraph (e.g. adverbs to link ideas or reference back to a point already made)	Commas to separate clauses
Use a range of verb prefixes for precision ('dis-', 'mis-', 'de-', 'over-', 're-')	Relative clauses beginning 'who', 'which', 'where', 'when', 'whose', 'that'	Using devices to link ideas across paragraphs (e.g. adverbials of time / tense choices)	Commas to separate relative clauses
Abstract nouns to describe human qualities or emotions ('courage', 'beauty', 'compassion', 'jealousy')	Relative clauses with an omitted relative pronoun	Managing pace with sentence length	Brackets / dashes for parenthesis
Adverbs to indicate likelihood or possibility ('perhaps', 'maybe', 'definitely')	Modal verbs to express possibility or obligation ('will', 'can', 'could', 'might', 'should', 'ought')	Editing balance of sentence length / sentence types to provide variety and interest across paragraph	Ellipses for omission
Metaphors / personification	Inserting a phrase beginning with an '-ing' verb (Ali ran on, panting with exhaustion, until he could go no further.)	Switching between past, present and future tenses as appropriate (in dialogue)	Commas to clarify meaning
Abstract nouns to give an air of authority ('charity', 'information', 'luxury', 'kindness')	Starting sentence with '-ed' verbs and adjectives (Frustrated and alone, Brian began the long walk home.)		Full speech punctuation including where speech is broken by other text
Alliteration / word play / puns	Rhetorical questions for effect		
	Greater range of fronted prepositional phrases ('At the very bottom of the sea,..', 'Far beyond the boundary of any map, …')		

Year Six

Word Level	Sentence Level	Paragraph Level	Punctuation
Vocabulary associated with formal and informal speech	Sentence structures typical of formal and informal speech	To manage text confidently, linking ideas both backwards and forwards	Commas for parentheses
Playing with a range of synonyms to achieve a precise effect	Active and passive voices	Link ideas across paragraphs using devices such as repetition of a word or phrase, grammatical connections or ellipsis	Commas to avoid ambiguity of meaning in sentences
Collective nouns	Subjunctive tense	Manage suspense by means of pace and omitted / surprise information	Colon to introduce lists and semi-colons within lists
Creating antonyms using prefixes		Use of flashback and flashforward	Colon to mark boundary between two related clauses
Hyphens to avoid ambiguity in compound words ('man-eating shark', 'a well-liked man')		Link the end of a text to the beginning	Semi-colon to mark boundary between two contrasting clauses
		Use a range of layout devices (bullet points, tables etc.) to structure text effectively	Dash to mark boundary between clauses

References

1. Crystal, D. (1996) Discover Grammar

2. Crystal, D. (2004) Rediscover Grammar

3. DfE (2014) National Curriculum

4. DfE (2012) Research Evidence for Writing

5. Ings, R. Writing is Primary – Action Research on the Teaching of Writing in Primary Schools

6. Lyons, L.S. (2006) Elements of Debating

7. McCormick Calkins, L. (1998) The Art of Teaching Writing

8. Myhill, D. (2005) Talking, listening, learning: Effective Talk in the Primary Classroom

9. Myhill, D. (2016) Essential Primary Grammar

10. OFSTED (2012) Moving English Forward

11. OFSTED (2003) Yes he Can – Schools Where Boys Write Well

12. OFSTED (2005) Messages on Improving Boys' Writing

Index

Adverbs 108, 148
Adverbial phrases 107
Art 127

Characters 21
Characterisation 23, 118
Classroom management 138
Clauses 101
Coherence 113
Cohesion 113
Conjunctive adverbs 147

Debating 18
Dialogue 118
Differentiation 58, 83
Drama / role-play 17

Environment 128

Feedback 132
Films 14
First draft 48
Free writing 32

Genre 29, 155
Geography 125

History 124

Idea tree 63

Marking 132
Mood 117
Morphology 33

Noun phrases 95

Paragraphs 118
PHSE 129
Planning 44, 59
Progression 167
Proof reading 55
Publishing 55
Punctuation 33

RE 128
Recount 64
Redraft 53, 121
Review 51

Scaffolding 58
Science 126
Settings 26
Sentences 99
Sentence bingo 77, 102
Sentence openers 105
Sentence stems 16
SPaG test 35
Spidergram 61
Standard English 17
Story boards 70
Story road map 66
Story structure 22, 24
Syntax 33

Telling / showing 93, 149
Transitional words and phrases 79, 115

Verbs 91
Viewpoint 25, 117
Vocabulary 18, 73, 88, 92

Writing for real purposes 130
Writing frames 80
Writing process 40